The Very Best Name for Baby

The Very Best Name for Baby

by Barbara Shook Hazen

Over 5,000 names for boys and girls—
plus a storehouse of inspiration
to help you choose

The C. R. Gibson Company, Norwalk, Connecticut 06856

Acknowledgements

CURTIS BROWN, LTD., for "My Name" by Lee Bennett Hopkins from
Kim's Place. Reprinted by permission of Curtis Brown, Ltd., Text
Copyright © 1974 by Lee Bennett Hopkins.

THE NEW YORK TIMES COMPANY for a quote by Barbara Walters
and a quote by Tammy Grimes from "By Any Other Name" by Jerome
Agel, November 28, 1976. Copyright © 1976 by The New York Times
Company. Reprinted by permission.

What Will You Name Your Baby?

Your baby's name is the first, and most meaningful, gift you will ever give your child. It is a gift for a lifetime.

Your baby's name is the identifying word the world will use to separate him or her from others—in school, on the playground, or in a pile of resumes. It is, conversely, the word that will link your child to others, in friendship and in affection.

Spoken names are the connectors that add personal warmth to such familiar human greetings as "Good morning," and "Hello." Written names are the labels for all your child's efforts, from first drawings and Mother's Day cards to school papers, love letters and book jackets.

Choosing the very best name for baby can be confusing. There are so many possibilities and considerations. Names have such different sounds, auras and meanings. There also may be family pressure to carry on family naming traditions you don't truly like, or differences in what the two of you do like.

The purpose of this book is to help take the hassle out of baby naming. It suggests basic ground rules, others' examples and offers a full alphabetical list of name origins and meanings, plus the latest information on trends, traditions, nicknames, and special circumstances such as—surprise!—twins.

It is also meant to be a keepsake in itself, a memento of the shared joy of choosing the most important word you will ever choose: your baby's name.

Barbara Shook Hazen

1

The Ten Basic Considerations of Baby Naming

1. *Pick what truly pleases you,* not your friends or family members. There may have been nine generations of Ildons, but if you hate the name, don't use it.

2. *Get rhythm.* The basic rule is that first and last names should be of unequal syllables. Melissa Mari sounds better than Mary Mari; Peter Shook sounds better than Saul Shook.

As with most rules, there are exceptions. Mark Twain has an elegant, important sound because of the strong vowel sounds. And Susan Hazen simply sounds nice. The choice is always yours.

"Play" with middle names. John Carter Smith is easier on the ear than John Curt Smith. Jessica Georgianna Cassevetes is a hard-to-say mouthful while Jessica Anne Cassevetes flows to the last name.

3. *Sound around.* Speak prospective names aloud, to each other and to friends. Most people have special feelings for certain letters—the murmur of m, the lyricism of l, the clipped quality of b, t, and d. Concentrate on names beginning with the letters you instinctively gravitate toward.

4. *Avoid stereotypes.* Some names—such as Prudence, Daisy, Elmer, Harvey and Fanny—have specific and/or unfortunate associations. They tend to be typecast and bring up certain mental pictures: Prudence of heavy seriousness and Daisy of flippancy—and a Prudence who wants to be a popular singer or a Daisy applying for a research grant may regret their preconditioning names.

5. *Give an alternate route.* Giving a middle name and a first name with variants gives a growing child who really dislikes his or her name a chance to make changes without taking a totally different name. Thus a Barbara can lighten what she is called to Babs; a Hubert may switch to his middle name James, if he feels it reflects a truer self.

6. *Honor ethnic heritage if pride in your national background is a strong part of your value system,* especially if the name is not difficult to pronounce. Do keep in mind that any obviously ethnic name acts as a label, which can be good and bad. Do avoid the kind of ethnic confusion of a name like Pedro O'Malley or Françoise Pilchowski.

7. *Think twice before you cast an unusual spelling over your child's name.* Mari and Jeorge lead to lifetimes of questions and mis-addressed envelopes. On the other hand, Ethel casts quite a different aura from Ethelle, as does Jane from Jayne.

There *are* plusses. Grown children often like the distinction of an unusual spelling. As one Madelon says, "I thank my father every day for the special spelling of my name."

8. *Don't yoke your child with a joke.* Graham is a name, but not if your last name is Cracker. Also avoid names that are hard to say, and keep in mind that some names, like Ivan and Bernard, can correctly be pronounced two ways.

9. *Baby's name is for all the ages and stages of his or her life.* Avoid both the overbearing and the babyish.

10. Consider the auras and meanings of many names, and any relative suggestions. Then in making the final decision, *Follow your own deepest inclinations.*

My name is a symbol.
My name is a key
To the heart
And meaning of me —
All that I am
And ever may be.
　　　　Barbara Shook Hazen

Practice Living with a Given Name
Before You Give It for Good

Say it, write it, roll it on the tongue. Say it with "I love you." Try calling "Come Ann? Melissa? Susan? Francine? Jessica? Judith? Nan? Nadine?"

Tip: Try prospective names on friends, relatives, friends' babies.

Write out prospective initials. Victoria Inez Principal and Sally Ollen Bowring are both fine-sounding names. But, initially speaking, they send very different messages.

Every time I say your name,
Each syllable is sweet.
What's in your name? From head to toe,
A special you I greet.
　　　　　Barbara Shook Hazen

5

One Couple's Solution: Let Baby Choose

The parents couldn't decide. All they knew was they wanted a name beginning with "a" in remembrance of her sister. By the second day, the nurses tagged the baby "No Name," and the parents still couldn't decide.

So they let baby decide. They called her by each of the five prospective names, finally choosing the one *she* responded to—the made-up name Alina.

In years to come, when asked, "How did you get your name?" she will be able to answer, "I chose it, with a little help from my Mom and Dad."

A name is a kind of face whereby one is known.
Thomas Fuller

My Name

I wrote my name on the sidewalk
But the rain washed it away.

I wrote my name on my hand
But the soap washed it away.

I wrote my name on the birthday card
I gave to Mother today

And there it will stay
For Mother never throws

ANYTHING

of mine away!
    Lee Bennett Hopkins

"I like it!" is a good enough reason for a name.

What's In?

J is currently the top letter, with Jennifer, Jessica, Jason, Jonathan and John all popular. There is a trend toward Biblical names, and another toward one-of-a-kind made-up names. Combination names such as Marjo (Mary + Joseph) and Charlanne (Charles + Ann) are in, reflecting a desire to honor both parents equally. Casual names are also in, reflecting a desire for informality. Also there is an increasing tendency to use variants such as Lisa, Wendy and Viki on birth certificates rather than the full, more formal Elizabeth, Wendolyn and Victoria.

What Does It Matter? Having a popular first name can be confusing if there are three other Jessicas in first grade.

However, it can also be reassuring because, according to psychological studies, popular names predispose teachers and strangers to positive thinking. Jessica and Jason are "expected" to do better and be more popular than Elmo and Prudence and, consequently, are treated more favorably, which makes the prophesy self-fulfilling.

(On the other hand, many a child has grown self-assertive and honed his sense of humor because of a "funny" name. And a name that affects a fourth-grader as embarrassingly different may be a source of distinction and pride to its owner as an adult.)

Naming Traditions

Jewish children are traditionally named for a worthy family member who is no longer alive, and often have both a secular and a purely Hebrew given name.

Christian, particularly Catholic, babies are traditionally given a saint's name at baptism as one of two given names. The saint then becomes a kind of spiritual mentor, model and protector. The feast day of the saint then may become a special day of remembrance, like a birthday.

Japanese children may be given names that indicate birth order. Ichiko, for instance, is number one child.

First Greek sons are frequently named after the grandfather.

Russian sons often take their father's name plus "ovich." Thus Michail Ivanovich, plus last name, has a father named Ivan.

American Indian names are believed to reflect their bearer's soul, and are deeply personal, often reflecting nature as in Laughing Water.

African Ashanti children named for the days of the week tend to live up (or down) to their names. Wednesday's child is expected to be feistier and more aggressive and does indeed, statistically end up in school trouble and jail more often.

Puritan children were given God-fearing names such as Obedience and Repentance in the hope that their behavior would reflect their good and godly names.

Namesake Notes

"Dear Abby" once said, "Phooey on these Juniors," when a mother wrote her lamenting "Bill" trouble, as "Little Bill" outgrew "Big Bill," creating personal embarrassment and many a crisis in the mail.

Naming the son after the father is an Anglo-Saxon custom, which some consider upper-crust, but which seems to have its down side. The minuses are that you may saddle your child with a name you never liked and he won't either, or that, having the exact same name makes it harder to forge and assert his separate identity.

The plusses are the sense of continuing past family tradition, bonding father and son in the present, and insuring that the name, as is, will live on.

Jewish parents generally do *not* name a child after a living relative. This harkens back to the prophet, Judah, who long ago warned that a man's soul might be deprived of rest if another were named after him in his own lifetime.

It is Greek tradition to create a hereditary chain by naming the grandson after the grandfather, which also creates less in-house confusion.

Fusion names are an effective way to honor both family sides. For example, preacher Marjoe Gortner's first name was a combination of Mary and Joseph. Marlyn honors Aunt Mary and Aunt Lynette. Joselle reflects Joseph and Ellen; Marlu combines Mark and Lucille.

To name a son after his mother: Most often the mother's maiden name, if attractive in fit and sound, is used as a middle name. Or the name can be given a male suffix. Thus Mary becomes Marle or Martley.

To name a girl after her mother: Use a variant of the name. For example, Mary might be changed to Maria, Marissa or Maryann. Ann's daughter might be Anita, Annabelle or Annette.

To name a girl after her father: Add a feminine ending. John's daughter thus becomes Joni or Jonette or Joanne. Edwin's daughter becomes Edwina, and Nicholas' daughter becomes Nicole.

Made-up Names

A today trend is toward made-up names that express individuality and/or hidden personal meanings. Such first names are most effectively combined with traditional middle names and "common" last names such as Smith or Jones.

Switched-around letters make anagram names such as Cepea (Peace) and Pentley (Plenty).

Switched-around syllables turn traditional Mary into Ryma, Gerald into Aldger, Dahlai into Liadah.

Telescope names may reflect deep-felt concerns such as ecology in Tesa (trees, earth, streams and air). Or the new name may be telescoped as a way to honor a well-known person—as in Marlu for Martin Luther King and Kenrob for Robert Kennedy.

Syllables may be played with until a nice-sounding combination is happened upon. If you like J sounds, put Jen-, Jess-, Jill- and Jul- on the left side of a piece of paper. On the right, try a variety of second syllables, resulting in Jenra, Jessita, Julard, among infinite possibilities.

Letters and/or syllables may be dropped to make Nicol out of Nicholas, Tilda out of Matilda, and Beth or Eliza from Elizabeth.

Make a little list of all the possibilities and their nicknames. Carry it everywhere with you, so you can add any names you happen upon at parties or on the bus.

Thrice happy he whose name has been well spelt.
Lord Byron

Her Name

In search from "A" to "Z" they passed,
And "Marguerita" chose at last;
But thought it sounded far more sweet
To call the baby "Marguerite."
When grandma saw the little pet,
She called her "darling Margaret."
Next Uncle Jack and Cousin Aggie
Sent cup and spoon to "little Maggie."
And grandpapa the right must beg
To call the lassie "bonnie Meg";
(From "Marguerita" down to "Meg")
And now she's simply "little Peg."
      Anonymous

Circumstantial Naming

Babies' names are sometimes chosen because of an event that occurred around the time of birth, or because of one or both of the parents' preoccupation with a profession, political feeling, place, or birth order.

Tidal Waters was born during a Florida hurricane. *Angel Levine* was so named because there were Angelus bells ringing during her birth. *Noel, Natalie* and *Holly* are names frequently given to Christmas babies. *April, May* and *June* denote spring babies. *Lyris* was the name given a girl child whose father is a musician and whose mother likes "l" sounds.

Missouri Compromise Jones (called Missy) and *Union Forever Shook* (Una) carved normal lives and nice nicknames out of Southern statement names. More recently, a California girl was named *Equal Rights Amendment* (Equa).

Portland James was named for her actor parents' favorite city and *Lorraine* reflects a much fought over French-German border.

Primus and *Primo* are often given Italian first-born boys; *Ultimus*, last-born. Some families have simplified naming to the bare bones of *First, Second, Third,* and *Lastly.*

Biblical Names

The Bible is a splendid source of resonant, interesting and unusual names as well as well-known traditional ones. Bathabara and Azriel are girls' names that mean "ferry house," and "help of God"; Jabal and Iram are boys' names that mean "stream" and "city."

A random opening of the Old Testament to Chronicles 1, verse 22 revealed the following names in less than a quarter of a page:

BOYS

Onam (Strong)
Jair (Enlightener)
Tekoah (Trumpet)
Michir (A seller)
Gilead (A witness)

GIRLS

Zaza (Prominent)
Bunah (Understanding)
Abihail (Exhultation-Abigail)

The Hebrew ending "El" stands for God. Thus, names such as Michael, Adiel, Manuel, Daniel and Gabriel, plus their feminine forms Michelle, Adiella, Manuella, Danielle and Gabrielle literally have "God" in them.

A good name is rather to be chosen than great riches.
        Proverbs 22:1

Boy/Girl Names

Evelyn, Vivien, Marion, Leslie, Joyce, Jesse, Noel, Sidney, Darsey and Harper are a few of the names spelled exactly the same for *both* sexes.

Many girls enjoy having names that span the sexes. They carry a kind of male prestige. When some jobs were tagged "men only," they were a plus on application forms.

What about boys with girlish names? Winston Churchill hated being called Winnie as a child. But by adulthood, he felt he grew in character and assertiveness *because* he grew stronger defending himself and his girlish name.

Similarly in the popular song, "A Boy Named Sue," a father, on purpose, gives his son a girl's name, so he'll better learn to defend himself—as did John Wayne, whose real given name was Marion, which landed him in girls' gym class and taught him to use his fists early.

Another solution, suggested by Ann Landers to a man whose wife was set on naming their son Vivien, is to call the child by his strong, strictly male second name or nickname: John or Jack, Michael or Mike.

Thought on Boy/Girl Naming

Boy babies are rarely given flippant names; girls frequently. This is partly custom and partly because girls are unfortunately still less thought of as world shapers. A girl whose given name is Daisy may take herself less seriously than a Margaret, who may informally and lovingly be called Daisy, but who uses her fuller, more formal name Margaret when she runs for office, or signs an important letter.

Whatever Name Works...Works

June Hamilton is a husky, good-humored, totally well-adjusted male sheriff in Lexington, Kentucky.

When asked, "Do you mind having a feminine name?" he answered, "No, why should I?"

When asked, "Obviously, you were born in June?" the reply was, "No, January."

June in January—happy with his name, and himself.

Twin Names

Over 60 percent of twins are given names that begin with the same initial: Mary and Mark, Jack and Jane, Sara and Star.

Twin names often balance in sound and number of syllables: Donald and Ronald, or Carolyn and Marylyn.

Existing but not recommended: Pete and Repeat, Kate and Duplicate.

Parents tend to give *identical* twins same sounding names, probably because the babies look and seem so much alike. Psychologists caution this may (but not necessarily) make it harder for Lisa and Liza to develop separate identities than if they were Lisa and Alison, whose names go well together but sound less like a team.

Name-Block and How to Get Over It

1. *Before* you go to sleep at night, program yourself to think of a half dozen or so good names first thing in the morning. Put a scratch pad on the wash basin to remind yourself. When you awake, write down the first names that float up from your subconscious.

2. List the friends' names you like to say best.

3. Ask your friends what they named their children, and why. (You may or may not agree with their choices. Either way will get you thinking.)

4. What would you want to be named if you could be named anew, and why?

5. Write a note to your unborn child. What name did you instinctively choose?

He's born in a good hour who gets a good name.
    Thomas Fuller

Early Deciders Versus Cliff Hangers

Some babies are named long before the fact: "Of course, if we ever have a boy, he'll be called Brian." Or "I can't wait to have a Jessica; I've always loved the name."

Others are given their names after much indecision, even, at times, after pressure from hospital nurses to "give the wee little one a name."

Both styles have their pitfalls. Early deciders should consider alternatives and name-shop around, to make sure the decision is based on a genuine liking for the name rather than handed down or habitual thinking.

Cliff hangers may have to tell themselves that, between several fine and fitting name choices, there are no "bad" decisions, just different ones. Then have the nurse hold straws.

Occasionally the unexpected happens at the hospital, where the birth name may be misspelled or at the christening, where the minister, handed the wrong side of the paper handed him by the nervous father, gave the newborn the whole string of "to be considered" names instead of *the* chosen one.

The use of last names began about the time of Columbus.
Before that, people were known by their first names and differentiated by descriptive phrase: John the bold, Ann the fair.

Many of today's first names (especially for boys) are also common last names such as Bryant, Stewart, James, Paul.

Last names make distinctive first names when they are pleasant-sounding and work well with the family name. They are out of the ordinary without being oddball, and are a good way to honor another side of the family.

Examples: Jackson Pollock, Freeman Brackett Hazen, Foster Smith, Emery Evans.

Nicknames

A nickname literally means "Ekename": an "also-name" used in place of the regular name.

It is not on the birth certificate, and it is not a new phenomena. Nicknames were used in ancient times when Ovid the poet was nicknamed "Flaccus," for flabby and Homer was called "The Prince of Poets."

In everyday life, nicknames often come from the way a person looks or acts. A Helen has been called Mickey all her life simply because she "looked like a little Mickey" in her crib. A Miranda has been called "Mouse" because one was her first and favorite plush toy.

But most often, nicknames are a variant or diminutive of the real name: Jack instead of John, Betty for Elizabeth, Arnie for Arnold. In the average first grade, probably half the children are called by a nickname—an important point to consider in choosing a name for baby. You may want Charles to stay Charles and deeply dislike Charlie and Chuck, but nicknames, like dandelions, have a way of happening outside of parental control.

Don't want your child to have a nickname? Look for a name that can't be changed—you hope.*

Examples for boys: Adam, Alan, Bart, Blake, Carl, Carson, Clark, Craig, Eric, Evan, Garth, Gary, Grant, Hugh, Joel, Kirk, Lance, Mark, Neal, Noah, Paul, Ross, Saul, Sean, Simon, Todd, Troy, Zane.

Examples for girls: Ann, April, Amber, Brooke, Carla, Dawn, Erin, Eve, Hazel, Jade, Joelle, Julie, June, Kara, Karen, Leigh, Lynn, Mia, Paige, Pearl, Sara, Zoe.

*(School children are notorious name changers and Bruce may, despite your efforts, end up Brucie, Joan end up Joansie or Joany-baloney and Amber-Amburger.)

"We chose *Connor*'s name so carefully," moaned the boy's mother, "because it was distinctive and couldn't be changed. And now, when the phone rings, I don't know whether his friends will ask for 'Connie,' 'Skinny,' or 'Con Man.'"

Nick Trick: to name so that the child's nickname and initials are the same. For example:

Kimberly Ida Muldoon = K.I.M.
Thomas Otto Morissey = T.O.M.

Most Popular Boys' Names

(As recorded in New York City Birth Certificates)

1984	1974	1964
1. Michael	Michael	Michael
2. Christopher	John	John
3. Daniel	Robert	Robert
4. David	David	David
5. Joseph	Christopher	Steven
6. Anthony	Anthony	Anthony
7. Jason	Joseph	William
8. Jonathan	Jason	Joseph
9. John	James	Thomas
10. Robert	Jose	Christopher*
		Richard*

1948	1928	1898
1. Robert	John	John
2. John	William	William
3. James	Joseph	Charles
4. Michael	James	George
5. William	Richard	Joseph
6. Richard	Edward	Edward
7. Joseph	Robert	James
8. Thomas	Thomas	Louis
9. Stephen	George	Francis
10. David	Louis	Samuel

Most popular boy's name ever? John in over two dozen varieties.

*Tied

Most Popular Girls' Names

(As recorded in New York City Birth Certificates)

1984	1974	1964
1. Jennifer	Jennifer	Lisa
2. Jessica	Michelle	Deborah
3. Melissa	Christine	Mary
4. Stephanie	Lisa	Susan
5. Nicole	Marie	Maria
6. Christina	Melissa	Elizabeth
7. Tiffany	Nicole	Donna
8. Danielle	Elizabeth	Barbara
9. Elizabeth	Jessica	Patricia
10. Lauren	Erica	Ann (e)*
		Theresa*

1948	1928	1898
1. Linda	Mary	Mary
2. Mary	Marie	Catherine
3. Barbara	Annie	Margaret
4. Patricia	Margaret	Annie
5. Susan	Catherine	Rose
6. Kathleen	Gloria	Marie
7. Carol	Helen	Esther
8. Nancy	Teresa	Sarah
9. Margaret	Joan	Frances
10. Diane	Barbara	Ida

All-time most popular girl's name? The grand old name Mary.

*Tied

Idaho Homegrown Names

In Idaho in 1984, there were two *Unique* baby girls, only one *Eve* for 325 *Adams*, and a gaggle of one-of-a-kind names including *Sir, Brie, Tansy, Ambrosia, Precious, Chance* and *Delight.*

Seventeen percent of the girls had unusual names while only ten percent of the boys did. Different spellings abounded with Nicholas taking top honors, having sixteen variations!

TOP 20 BOYS' NAMES

Rank	Name	Rank	Name
1.	Michael	11.	Adam
2.	Christopher	12.	James
3.	Matthew	13.	Nicholas
4.	Joshua	14.	Brandon
5.	Ryan	15.	Brian
6.	Daniel	16.	Justin
7.	David	17.	Robert
8.	Andrew	18.	John
9.	Joseph	19.	Tyler
10.	Jason	20.	Kyle

TOP 20 GIRLS' NAMES

Rank	Name	Rank	Name
1.	Jennifer	11.	Emily
2.	Jessica	12.	Amy
3.	Amanda	13.	Elizabeth
4.	Ashley	14.	Rachel
5.	Sarah	15.	Amber
6.	Melissa	16.	Crystal
7.	Stephanie	17.	Erin
8.	Nicole	18.	Angela
9.	Megan	19.	Kimberly
10.	Heather	20.	Rebecca

On the 19,654 certificates for newborn girls, the name Jennifer displaced Sarah as the most popular name. If both the names Sarah and Sara were counted together then it would place second in the ranking. Increasing in popularity were Ashley, Stephanie, Megan and Emily, while Amy, Erin, Kimberly, and Rebecca had declined as given names. Katherine would be in the top 10 given names if all 15 variations of its spellings were totaled.

Many parents have favorite names, but try to differentiate their child's name by a variation in spelling. Parents were more creative with the names they gave to their baby girls. Seventeen percent of 3,339 of the girls had unique names or one-of-a-kind spellings; whereas, boys had 2,009 (10 percent) unique names. Similarly, the top 15 male names account for 30 percent of all the boys' names, where the top 15 female names comprise only 23 percent of total girls' names.

Some parents have gone to greater lengths to give their child a special name: Sources of inspiration for parents often are based on geography or weather with names chosen such as Sacramento, Dallas, Laramie, Sierra, Nevada, Brooklyn, Savanah, Africa or Windy, Winter, Sunshine, Starlight, Rainbow and Sky. Two parents issued their sons titles with the names Dr and Sir. There was only 1 Eve for the 325 Adams. Of the 14 boys and girls named Noel or Noelle, only one was born on December 25, 1984. Other interesting names that caught the attention of our researchers were Attila, Thor, Rube, Snake, Justice, Fast, Dash, Tansy, Ambrosia, Brie, Briar, Chance, Delight, Jeopardy, Liberty, Pinky, Precious and Echo.

Blank or no first names were found on 338 certificates as a consequence of parental dispute or indecisiveness. Names can be *added* to birth certificates within one year of the filing date with no charge.

For the trivia buffs, other statistics from our data file show an average of 111 babies born every day in Oregon. The busiest day in the nursery was Tuesday, May 29 with 164 babies born. The slowest day, with only 66 babies, was Sunday, April 22.

Real Celebrity Names That Sound Staged

Robert Redford
Cliff Robertson
Alan Alda
Beau Bridges
Mia Farrow
Hayley Mills
Mary Pickford
Marlon Brando
Darryl Hickman

Charlie Chaplin
Sissy Spacek
Drew Barrymore
Meryl Streep
Candice Bergen
Madonna (named after her mother)
Swoozie Kurtz
Farrah Fawcett
Will Palmer

Increasingly actors opt to keep their real names, even those with less than musical monikers such as Larry Hagman and Cloris Leachman, who refused to change her name even when she was told she sounded like a laundry detergent.

John Uhler Lemmon III stoutly refused the efforts of Hollywood moguls to change his name. He could handle them, just as, in school, he'd handled being called "John U. Lemmon."

Star Babies

The names of star babies often have a dramatic flair.

Mick Jagger has *Jade* and Michelle Phillips has a *China*.

Mary Martin has a *Heller* and Tony Perkins has an *Osgood*.

Mia Farrow and Andre Previn produced a *Larksong* and a *Summer Song*.

Actress Faye Dunaway and photographer Terry O'Neill have a son *Liam*.

Ringo Starr's son is *Zak*, David Bowie's *Zowie*, and Elliot Gould has a *Sam Bazooka*.

Cher has a daughter *Chastity* and a son *Elijah Blue*.

David Carradine and Barbara Hershey's son's name is *Free*; Sylvester Stallone's *Sage Moonblood*.

Aretha L. Franklyn and Ken E. Cunningham co-produced an acronymous child *Kecalf* (a combination of all six initials).

Frank Zappa has four starshoots: Daughter *Moon Unit*, following in his musical footsteps, as well as *Dweezil, Diva* and *Ahmed Emuukha Rodan*!

A well-chosen name stands the test of time

Many children, particularly adolescents going through other changes, go through a period of wanting to change their name.

After questioning, most children settle in to liking and feeling like the names they were born with, as did actress Tammy Grimes, who once yearned to be a Fern, and television star Barbara Walters, who felt her true self was a Babs.

Tammy Grimes: There was a time, I must have been about sixteen, when I hadn't yet grown up to my face; I wanted to be called Fern or Scarlet—to me, much more romantic and exotic sounds than Tammy. But this passed after reading that Charles Dickens had called his chimney sweeps "Grimes"— and that seemed to make Tammy Grimes a good name. Scarlet or Fern Grimes would never do.

Barbara Walters: I used to hate my name. I thought it was boring. It sounded like those books I read when I was a little girl: Barbara Walters, Student Nurse. In school, every little girl wants to change her name. I wanted mine to be Babs Elliott (with two t's.) I thought it was so smart and elegant. But the closest I ever came to it was with my Boston aunt who, to this day, calls me "Babsy."

What *Not* To Name the Baby

Avoid anything that makes an unfortunate combination with the last name, such as John Paper, Rose Bush, Otto Mann, and Elly Funt.

Avoid rhyme names such as Jack Zack, Aaron Carron and Myrna Turner.

Avoid names with unfortunate initial possibilities, such as David Ulster Downs (D.U.D.), Harriet Ann Gregory (H.A.G.), and Isabelle Carin Kimball (I.C.K.).

Steer clearest of all of personal-meaning or joke names, like Encore for a little Jones who wasn't on the program.

Harveys United

Harvey is a first name with a checkered past, being an invisible rabbit in a play, and the butt of cartoon and commercial characters, where "Harveys" were portrayed as bumbling and fumbling.

But finally a New York public-relations Harvey got mad. He whipped off letters to 150 prominent Harveys (including pianist Harvey Van Cliburn and tire magnate Harvey Firestone) who shared his disgusted feelings about being portrayed as dolts. They formed a national pro-Harvey movement to upgrade the image of Harvey and to have the offensive commercials dropped. They were.

Mass-media-name-drop: When Jerry Lewis impersonated a fool named Melvin, there was a sharp drop in parents selecting that name.

The Big Six Reasons for Name Changing

1. Dislike.
2. Difficulty in spelling and/or pronunciation.
3. Embarrassment, as in Ima Bugg.
4. Ethnic confusion, as in Carmen O'Reilly.
5. Too common.
6. Too uncommon.

Want to be able to brag that your child can spell his or her name backwards? Give a name that's spelled the same both ways: Eve, Emme, Ede, Hannah, Otto, Ada, Ava, Nan and Ono (a Biblical girl's name that means strong).

"John Bull" is the term used for the typical Englishman. "John Doe" is used in legal documents when the real name is unknown. "Johnny Reb" is the term used to refer to a Confederate soldier. "Johnny Jump-up" is the name of a flower, "Johnny Cake" is a cake or bread made from corn meal. "Johnny on the Spot" refers to anyone who is always there at the right time. A "jack o'lantern" is a lighted pumpkin, and a "Jack of all trades" is someone who can do anything. "Johnny-come-lately" is a late arrival.

New Leaves from Older Branches

Heirloom names may be quaint, quirky, dignified or simply melodic. An heirloom name, particularly one plucked from your own family tree, is a nice way to honor ancestors and give today's child a gift from the past.

Here is a random nosegay of Eighteenth-Century names. Early birth names can best be found in court house records, or in the clippings and keepings of unofficial elderly family historians.

BOYS' NAMES	GIRLS' NAMES
Azariah	Abby
Caleb	Alma
Eben	Arletta
Ezra	Betsey
Freeman	Delia
Holis	Florence
Ichabod	Gussie
Jeremiah	Huldah
Jesse	Ida
Noah	Leona
Sylvanus	Mercy
Waldron	Rachel
Zebidiah	Viola

Other Names for Names

Moniker or *Monicker*: A slang expression for name or nickname.

Pen Name: Made-up name used by writers.

Pseudonym: A made-up name, whose main purpose is to conceal the real name.

Code Name: Short identifying name used mainly by spies and government officials.

Stage Name: The made-up name of an actor or actress, mainly chosen for memorability and appeal.

Sobriquet: Old-fashioned word for nickname and stage name.

Onomastics: The study of names.

"To make a name for yourself," is almost every parent's fond wish for his or her child, and is itself an expression that connects high hopes and a good name.

Word association is the memory trick that makes certain names like *May* and *Leo* easy to remember. (When you first meet *May*, you may picture bringing her spring flowers and when you first meet *Leo*, you may imagine him with a lion's mane.)

But tricks can backfire as a girl named *Hazel* was to find out all too well when she was told, "Your exact name's slipped my mind, but I know you're some kind of nut."

Lily? Ivy? Daffodil?
Fern or Violet for a girl?
To give a boy a green-thumb start,
Consider Moss as in Moss Hart.
　　　　Barbara Shook Hazen

Some names such as *April, May, June* and *Spring* are exactly the same as the nouns from which they are derived. Other names, such as *Dexter* and *Curtis*, are less obviously related: *Dexter* is from the Latin word dextrous, which means both right-handed and skilled with one's hands, while *Curtis* derives from the French word for courtesy. Thus, anyone named *Curtis Dexter* would be labeled both deft and polite.

Old Families—Old-Fashioned Names

A random survey of first names of young Rockefellers includes Victoria, Lawrence, Anne, Thomas, Michael, Elizabeth, Deborah, Shirley and a more modern Malinda.

A culling of young Cabots includes Emily, Charles, Marianne, Andrew, Christopher, Cornelia, Peter, John, David, Samuel and Chilton.

A mix of young Morgans includes Charles, Samuel, Eugenia, Anna, Wendy, Rose, John, Francesca, Katherine and four sisters with end in "a" names: Teresa, Eleanora, Cecilia and Maria.

Does a James by any other name do as well? Evidently not, according to a California psychological study in which the James and Williams of the world were rated more stable, responsible and "with it" than their familiar counterparts, the Jims and Bills, and still more kidlike, Jimmys and Billys.

A charity worker brought a poor fatherless boy named John Adamson into a clothing store. The clerk, sizing up the situation, brought out a cheap suit.

The boy looked crestfallen until the older man spoke up indignantly, "Bring out your best suit. Don't you recognize the boy? This is John Adamson!"

Keep saying if pressured by relatives,
"Our baby's name is ours to give."
Even if there were five Elberts before,
That's no edict for one more.
Tradition and family ties at best lie lightly,
Not bind tightly.
  Barbara Shook Hazen

The Very Best Names
For Baby Boys

Key to abbreviations used in the following pages

American Indian *(Am.Ind.)*
Anglo-Saxon *(AS)*
Arabic *(A)*
Aramaean *(Ar)*
Celtic *(C)*
Danish *(Da)*
Egyptian *(Eg)*
English *(E)*
French *(F)*
French-Celtic *(FC)*
French-Latin *(FL)*
Gaelic *(Ga)*
Greek *(G)*
Hebrew *(H)*
Hebrew-Latin *(HL)*
Italian *(It)*
Japanese *(J)*
Latin *(L)*
Middle English *(ME)*

Norse *(N)*
Old English *(OE)*
Old French *(OF)*
Old French Latin *(OFL)*
Persian *(P)*
Russian *(Russ)*
Sanskrit *(San)*
Saxon *(Sa)*
Scandinavian *(Sc)*
Slavonic *(Sl)*
Spanish *(Sp)*
Spanish-Arabic *(SpA)*
Spanish-Latin *(SpL)*
Swiss *(Sw)*
Teutonic *(T)*
Teutonic-Latin *(TL)*
Uncertain *(U)*
Welsh *(W)*

A

Aaron *(H)*	a mountain; tower of strength	Alcott *(C)*	from the stone cottage
Abbot *(H)*	father	Alden *(OE)*	old friend
Abel *(H)*	breath	Aldous *(T)*	old; wise
Abelard *(T)*	resolute; ambitious	Aldrich *(T)*	king
Abner *(H)*	paternal; bright	Alexander *(G)*	
Abraham *(H)*	tall; father of many	Alex	leader; defender of
Absolom *(H)*	peace loving	Alec	men
Achilles *(G)*	taciturn; sympathetic	Alfred *(OE)*	of good counsel; kingly
Adair *(C)*	from the oaktree ford		
Adam *(H)*	man	Alger *(AS)*	spearman
Addison *(AS)*	Adam's descendant	Algernon *(F)*	prosperous
Adelbert *(T)*	mentally brilliant	Alison *(T)*	of holy fame
Adin *(H)*	sensual	Alonzo *(G)*	ready; willing
Adlai *(H)*	just	Aloysius *(L)*	Grace
Adolph *(T)*	noble hero	Alphonse *(T)*	ready for battle
Adonis *(G)*	handsome	Alston *(OE)*	from the old manor
Adrian *(L)*	pessimistic; man of the sea coast	Alton	or village
		Alva *(H)*	tall
Ahab *(H)*	uncle	Alvin *(T)*	noble friend; beloved of all
Ahern *(C)*	Lord of the horses		
Ahearn		Ambrose *(G)*	immortal
Ainsley *(OE)*	of a nearby meadow	Amery *(T)*	
Alan *(C)*		Amory	industrious
Allan	cheerful; in harmony	Amos *(H)*	strong; courageous
Allen		Anatole *(G)*	of the East
Allyn		Andrew *(G)*	
Alaric *(T)*	ruler of all	Andre	manly
Alastair		Andy	
Allister *(G)*	see Alexander	Angelo *(G)*	angel; messenger
Alaster		Angus *(C)*	exceptional
Alban *(L)*	white	Anselm *(T)*	divine helmet of God
Albin		Ansley *(OE)*	from the awe-inspiring pasture, meadow
Albert *(T)*	firm; responsible; noble	Anson *(AS)*	son of Ann

Anthony *(L)* ⎫
Antonio ⎬ incomparable;
Antony ⎭ praiseworthy
Archibald *(T)* ⎫ holy prince; extremely
Archie ⎭ bold
Arden *(L)* eager; sincere
Armand *(F)* public spirited
Armstrong
(OE) with a strong arm
Arne *(Sc)* eagle
Arno *(T)* eagle
Arnold *(T)* strong as an eagle
Arthur *(C)* high-minded; strong
as a rock

Arvid *(Sc)* eagle forest
Arvin *(T)* friend of the people
Asa *(H)* healer
Asher *(H)* fortunate
Ashley *(AS)* dweller in the ash tree
meadow
Aubrey *(T)* ruler of the elves
Auburn *(U)* fine-appearing
August *(L)* ⎫ venerable majestic;
Augustus *(L)* ⎭ imperial
Austin *(L)* useful
Averill *(AS)* of April
Axel *(H)* man of peace

Sibling Suites

There are many unifying threads to tie siblings together:

1. Use of the same opening letter in the names; such as, Robert, Randy, Ruth, Rolisa and Russell.

2. Use of the same ending, as in Maria, Sofia, and Tesia.

3. Use of a rhymed ending as in Mack and Zack, or Ann, Nan and Jan.

4. Use of unifying interest as in Ertha, Ariadne and Oceanna.

B

Bailey *(OF)* }
Baylen } Bailiff or steward

Baird *(C)* — bard or minstrel
Baldwin *(T)* — friendly; bold
Bancroft *(AS)* — from the bean field
Barclay — see Berkeley
Barlow *(OE)* — dweller on the bare hill

Barnet — see Bernard
Barnaby *(H)* — son of consolation
Barrett *(T)* — bear-like
Barrie *(C)* }
Barry } straight-forward

Bartholomew }
Bart *(H)* } warlike son

Baruch *(H)* — blessed
Basil *(G)* — royal
Bayard *(F)* — of fiery hair
Baxter *(OE)* — baker
Benedict *(L)* — blessed
Benjamin *(H)* }
Ben }
Bennie } son of the right hand; surety
Benny }

Bennett — see Benedict
Benton *(AS)* — of the moors
Berkeley *(AS)* — from the birch meadow

Bernard *(T)* }
Bernhard } bold as a bear
Bernie }

Bert *(T)* }
Bertram } bright

Beverley *(AS)* — from the beaver meadow

Bevan *(C)* }
Bevin } son of Evan

Bill }
Billie } see William
Billy }

Blaine *(C)* — thin or lean
Blair *(C)* — a place
Blake *(OE)* — fair-haired
Bob }
Bobby } see Robert

Booth *(T)* — home lover
Borden *(OE)* — he lives near the boar's den

Boris *(Sl)* — warrior
Bowen *(C)* — son of Owen
Boyd *(C)* — yellow-haired
Bradford *(AS)* — from the broad ford
Bradley *(AS)* — from the broad meadow

Bramwell *(OE)* — of Abraham's well
Brand *(U)* — a fighter
Brant *(T)* — firebrand
Brendan *(C)* — from the lighted hill
Brent *(OE)* — from the steep hill
Brett *(C)* — a Breton
Brewster *(OE)* — brewmaster
Brian *(C)* — strong; sincere
Brice *(C)* — ambitious
Brigham *(OE)* — dweller by the bridge
Bromely *(OE)* — dweller in the meadow

Brock *(C)* — badger
Bruce *(Ga)* — positive; daring
Bruno *(T)* — brown

Bryan	} see Brian
Bryant	
Bryce *(C)*	ambitious
Burgess *(T)*	a townsman

Burke *(T)*	from the castle
Burl *(OE)*	cup bearer
Burton *(AS)*	of bright fame
Byron *(T)*	from the cottage

C

Cadwallader *(Sc)*	valiant in war
Cadman *(C)*	brave warrior
Caesar *(L)*	purposeful
Calder *(C)*	from the river of stones
Caleb *(H)*	a dog lover
Calvert *(OE)* Calbert	} herdsman
Calvin *(L)*	bold
Camden *(G)*	from the winding valley
Cameron *(C)*	crooked nose
Campbell *(F)*	from a bright field
Canute *(N)*	knot
Carew *(C)*	from this fortress
Carey	see Charles
Carl *(T)*	forceful
Carleton *(T)* Charleton	} of Charles' farm
Carlisle *(OE)* Carlyle	} from the walled city
Carlos	see Charles
Carmen *(L)*	song
Carroll *(C)* Carrol	} champion
Carson *(W)*	his father lives near marshes

Carter *(OE)*	cart-driver
Carver *(AS)*	carver
Cary *(C)* Carey	} from the fortress
Casey *(C)*	valorous
Casimir *(Sl)*	proclamation of peace
Caspar *(Sa)*	gift-bearer
Cecil *(Sa)*	harmony
Cedric *(C)*	chieftain
Chadwick *(OE)*	from the warrior's town; defender
Chandler *(F)*	candlemaker
Channing *(AS)*	knowing
Chapin *(F)*	man of gold
Charles *(T)*	manly; man of the people
Chauncey *(F)*	official record-keeper
Chester *(OE)* Cheston	} dweller in a fortified town
Chilton *(AS)*	from the farm by the spring
Christian *(L)*	Christian
Christopher *(G)*	Christ-bearer
Clarence *(L)*	bright; illustrious
Clark *(L)* Clarke	} wise
Claude *(L)*	affectionate

Clay *(T)*	man of clay or mortal	Conway *(C)*	man of the great plains
Clayton *(T)*	from the town on the clay bed	Coolidge *(U)*	careful and protective
Clement *(L)*	merciful	Corbin *(L)*	} the raven
Clifford *(Sa)*	valorous	Corwin	
Clifton *(OE)*	from the farm at the cliff	Cornelius *(L)*	studious; noble
Clinton *(T)*	from the headland farm	Courtland *(AS)*	from the enclosed land or court
Clive *(OE)*	cliff dweller	Courteney *(F)*	a place
Clyde *(W)*	heard from afar	Craig *(S)*	crag dweller
Colby *(OE)*	from the black farm	Crandall *(OE)*	of the valley of the cranes
Cole	form of Nicholas	Crawford *(OE)*	of the crow's ford
Colin *(C)*	strong; young and virile	Crosby *(T)*	dweller by the town cross
Coleman *(C)*	} dove	Crosley *(OE)*	from the meadow with a cross
Colman			
Columbus *(G)*	curious	Culbert *(T)*	noted; bright
Conal *(C)*	} high and mighty	Culver *(OE)*	dove
Conan		Curt *(L)*	short or little
Conrad *(T)*	bold counsel; resolute	Curtis *(OF)*	courteous
Conroy *(C)*	wise	Cyril *(G)*	lordly
Constantine *(L)*	unwavering	Cyrus *(P)*	throne

D

Dag *(Sc)*	day of brightness	Dan *(H)*	judge
Dale *(T)*	dweller in the dale	Dana *(Sc)*	} a Dane
Dallas *(C)*	spirited	Dane	
Dalton *(OE)*	from the farm in the dale	Daniel *(H)*	God has judged
Damon *(G)*	tame	Darcy *(C)*	dark; dweller in the stronghold

41

Darius *(P)*   dark; strong

Darrell *(OE)*
Daryl
Darren   beloved; dear

David *(H)*   beloved

Davin *(Sc)*   bright man

Davis *(OE)*   contraction of David's son

Dean *(OE)*
Deane   from the valley

Dearborn *(AS)*   beloved child

Delano *(OF)*   from the place of nut trees

Delbert *(T)*   bright and noble

Delmar *(L)*   of the sea

Demetrius *(G)*   lover of the earth

Denby *(Sc)*   loyal Dane

Denis *(G)*
Dennis
Denny   worshipper

Derek *(T)*
Dirk   ruler of the people

Desmond *(C)*   sophisticated

Dewey *(U)*   controlled physical power

Dexter *(L)*   fortunate

Dillon *(C)*   faithful and true

Dion *(G)*   short for Dionysos, God of wine

Doane *(C)*   from the sand hill or dune

Dominic *(L)*
Dominick   belonging to the Lord

Don *(C)*
Donal
Donald
Donnie
Donovan   world ruler

Dorian *(G)*   from Dori

Douglas *(C)*
Douglass   thoughtful

Doyle *(C)*   dark stranger

Drake *(ME)*   owner of the dragon inn

Drew *(T)*   honest

Driscoll *(C)*   the interpreter

Duane *(C)*   singing

Dudley *(OE)*   from the town of Dudley

Duke *(L)*   leader

Duncan *(C)*   brown chief

Dunstan *(AS)*   from the brown stone hill

Dunton *(OE)*   of the farm over the hill

Durand *(L)*   lasting friend

Durward *(AS)*   the door keeper

Dwaine
Dwayne   see Duane

Dwight *(T)*   white; fair

Dylan *(W)*
Dilan
Dilly   from the sea

Might weather caster Storm Field *have been a zoologist had his given name been* Wolfgang? *A farmer had it been* Wheatley? *Or a member of the military had it been* Warren?

42

E

Earl *(OE)*	} noble warrior
Earle	
Eaton *(AS)*	of the river
Eben *(H)*	stone
Ebenezer *(H)*	stone of help
Edan *(C)*	flame
Edgar *(OE)*	wealthy
Edmond *(OE)*	} protector of wealth
Edmund	
Edric *(AS)*	rich ruler
Edsel *(AS)*	prosperous
Edward *(OE)*	guardian of wealth
Edwin *(OE)*	friend of wealth
Egan *(T)*	formidable
Egbert *(T)*	precocious; bright
Elbert *(T)*	overpowering; illustrious
Elden *(T)*	} respected
Eldon	
Eldridge *(AS)*	} wise advisor
Eldwin	
Eleazar *(H)*	helped by God
Eli *(H)*	highest
Elias *(H)*	} faithful to God
Elihu	
Elijah	
Ellery *(T)*	of the alder trees
Eliot	
Eliott	} see Elias
Elliott	
Ellis	
Elson	son of Elias
Ellsworth *(AS)*	lover of the earth
Elmer *(AS)*	excellent; famous
Elmo *(G)*	lovable; friendly
Elroy *(L)*	royal

Elton *(AS)*	from the old farm
Elvin	see Alvin
Elvis *(N)*	wise
Elwin *(AS)*	
Elwood	} friend of the elves
Elwyn	
Emmanuel *(H)*	God is with us
Emerson *(T)*	son of Emery
Emery *(T)*	} dutiful
Emory	
Emil *(T)*	} industrious
Emile	
Emmett *(AS)*	} diligence
Emmet	
Enoch *(H)*	teacher
Enos *(H)*	mortal man
Ephraim *(H)*	very fruitful
Erasmus *(G)*	amiable
Eric *(T)*	
Erich	} princely
Erik	
Erland *(T)*	noble eagle
Ernest *(G)*	serious
Errol *(T)*	a nobleman
Ervin	} see Irwin
Erwin	
Esmond *(AS)*	gracious protector
Ethan *(H)*	strength; steadfast
Eugene *(G)*	well-born
Evan *(E)*	challenger
Evelyn *(OE)*	a dear youth
Everard	} mighty as a boar
Everett *(T)*	
Ewald *(L)*	bearer of good news
Ezekiel *(H)*	God's strength
Ezra *(H)*	dawn, beginning of joy

F

Fabian *(L)*	prosperous farmer
Fairbanks *(U)*	sympathetic
Fairfax *(AS)*	fair-haired
Fairley *(AS)*	from the far meadow
Falkner *(AS)* Faulkner	} trainer
Farand *(T)*	attractive
Farley *(AS)*	from the far meadow
Farrell *(C)* Farrel	} man of valor
Favian *(L)*	man of understanding
Faxon *(T)*	famous for his hair
Felix *(L)*	fortunate; happy
Fenton *(AS)*	dweller of the marshland
Ferdinand *(T)* Fernand	} adventurous
Fergus *(C)*	strong man
Ferris *(C)*	rock
Firman *(AS)*	traveler to far places
Fisk *(Sc)*	fisherman

Flavian *(L)*	blond; fair-haired
Fletcher *(F)*	arrow-maker
Fleming *(AS)*	Dutchman
Florian *(L)*	flowering
Floyd *(C)*	the gray
Forrest *(T)* Forest	} from the woods
Foster *(T)*	keeper of the woods
Franchot *(T)*	the free
Francis Frank *(T)*	} free
Franklin *(T)* Franklyn	} free man
Frederick *(T)* Frederic Fredrick Fredric Fritz	} peaceful ruler
Freeman *(AS)*	one born free
Fulton *(AS)*	from a farm

Any name that you cherish
spoken with love
will grow to fit
your child like a glove.
  Barbara Shook Hazen

44

G

Gabriel *(H)* — man of God
Gadman *(H)* — the fortunate
Gail *(C)*
Gale } lively, gay
Galen *(G)* — healer
Galvin *(C)* — the sparrow
Gamaliel *(H)* — the Lord is my recompense

Garett *(T)*
Gareth
Garreth } mighty with the spear
Garrett
Garland *(OF)* — crowned for victory
Garner *(T)* — the defender; protecting warrior
Garnet *(L)* — red jewel
Garrick *(T)* — mighty warrior
Garth *(AS)* — yard-keeper
Garvin *(T)* — friend in battle
Gawain *(T)*
Gavin } battle hawk
Gaylord *(AS)* — joyous noble
Geoffrey *(T)* — God's peace; brave
George *(G)* — farmer
Gerald *(T)* — dominion with the spear
Gerard *(T)* — mighty with the spear
Gervase *(T)* — honorable

Gideon *(H)* — the deliverer
Gifford *(T)* — gift
Gilbert *(T)* — bright pledge; progressive
Giles *(L)* — shield bearer
Gilroy *(L)* — king's servant
Glein *(C)* — from the valley
Glen *(C)*
Glenn } from the valley or glen
Goddard *(T)* — firm in nature
Godfrey *(T)* — quiet
Goodwin *(T)* — good and faithful friend
Gordon *(Ga)* — generous
Graham *(T)* — from the gray home
Grant *(L)* — great
Granville *(F)* — of the great town
Gregory *(G)* — vigilant
Griffin *(L)* — mythical beast
Griffith *(L)* — having great faith
Griswold *(T)* — from the wild gray forest
Grover *(AS)* — grove-dweller
Gunther *(T)* — bold warrior
Gustave *(Sc)* — noble staff
Guthrie *(C)* — war serpent
Guy *(F)* — leader; guide

As his name is, so is he.
1 Samuel 25:25

H

Hadley *(OE)*	from the heath
Hal	see Henry
Halbert *(C)*	gentleman
Hale *(T)*	robust
Hall *(OE)*	from the master's house
Halsey *(AS)*	from Hal's island
Hamilton *(F)*	from the beautiful mountain
Harcourt *(F)*	from the armed court
Hardy *(T)*	of hardy stock
Harlan *(T)*	from the land of warriors
Harland	
Harley *(AS)*	from the hare's meadow
Harod *(H)*	loud terror
Harold *(AS)*	commander of the army
Harrison *(OE)*	noble
Hart	from the deer's meadow
Hartley *(AS)*	
Harvey *(C)*	bitter
Hayden *(T)*	from the hedged hill
Hayes *(OE)*	from the woods
Hector *(G)*	unswerving; steadfast
Helmut *(G)*	helmet of courage
Henry *(T)*	ruler of the home
Herbert *(T)*	illustrious warrior
Herman *(T)*	warrior
Herrod *(H)*	heroic conqueror
Herwin *(T)*	friend
Heywood *(T)*	from the dark green forest
Hezekiah *(H)*	God is strength
Hilary *(L)*	cheerful; merry
Hillary	
Hilliard *(T)*	protector
Hiram *(H)*	nobly born
Hobart *(G)*	having a bright mind
Hobey	
Holbrook *(AS)*	from the valley brook
Holden *(T)*	kind
Hollis *(AS)*	dweller by the holly trees
Holman *(T)*	from the river island
Homer *(G)*	pledge; secure
Horace *(L)*	timekeeper; worthy to be beheld
Horatio	
Hosea *(H)*	salvation
Howard *(T)*	chief guardian
Hubert *(T)*	bright in spirit; intellectual
Hugh *(T)*	mind, intelligence
Hugo	
Humbert *(T)*	bright home
Hume *(T)*	lover of his home
Humphrey *(T)*	protector of the peace
Hunter *(OE)*	a hunter
Hyman *(H)*	life

I

Ian	see John	Irvin *(AS)*	
Ichabod *(H)*	the glory has departed	Irving	friend of the sea
Ignatius *(L)*	fiery and ardent	Irwin	
Igor *(Sc)*	hero	Isaac *(H)*	mirthful; glad
Ingram *(T)*	the raven	Isidore *(G)*	gift
Inness *(C)*	from the island	Israel *(H)*	the Lord's soldier
Ira *(H)*	watchful	Ivar *(Sc)*	archer

J

Jabez *(H)*	cause of sorrow	Jethro *(H)*	outstanding
Jack	see John	Joab *(H)*	praise the Lord
Jacob *(H)*	the supplanter	Joachim *(H)*	the Lord will judge
James		Job *(H)*	the afflicted
Jared *(H)*	descendant	Jock	see John
Jarvis *(T)*	sharp as a spear	Joel *(H)*	Jehovah is God
Jason *(G)*	healer	John *(H)*	God is gracious; given
Jasper *(P)*	bringer of treasure	Jonathan	by God
Jay *(AS)*	crow, or lively	Jonah *(H)*	place
Jeconiah *(H)*	gift of the Lord	Jonas *(H)*	dove
Jedediah *(H)*	beloved by the Lord	Jordan *(H)*	descending
Jeffrey	see Geoffrey	Joseph *(H)*	he shall add
Jegar *(H)*	witness our love	Joses *(H)*	helped by the Lord
Jerald	see Gerald	Joshua *(H)*	Jehovah saves
Jeremiah *(H)*		Josiah *(H)*	he is healed by the
Jeremy	exalted by the Lord		Lord
Jermyn		Jotham *(H)*	God is perfect
Jerome *(G)*	having a holy name; exalted	Julius *(L)*	kind
		Julian	
Jesse *(H)*	God's grace	Justin *(L)*	just

K

Kane *(C)*	bright; radiant	Kenway *(AS)*	brave soldier
Karl	see Charles	Kenyon *(C)*	fair-haired
Kay *(E)*	strong; determined	Kermit *(C)*	free
Keane *(OE)*	} sharp; tall; handsome	Kerr *(C)*	dark; mysterious
Keene		Kerry *(C)*	} the dark
Keith *(W)*	wood-dweller	Keary	
Kelby *(T)*	} from the farm	Kevin *(C)*	kind; gentle
Kilby	by the spring	Kimball *(AS)*	royally brave
Kelly *(U)*	impetuous; gentle and helpful	Kingsley *(AS)*	from the king's meadow
Kelsey *(T)*	} dweller by the water	Kirby *(T)*	} from the church village
Kelcey		Kerby	
Kendall *(C)*	} chief of the valley	Kirk *(Sc)*	living close to the church
Kendal			
Kendrick *(AS)*	royal ruler	Knute *(Da)*	kind
Kenelm *(AS)*	bright helmet	Kurt *(G)*	German form of Conrad
Kenley *(OE)*	of the king's meadow		
Kenneth *(C)*	handsome	Kyle *(Ga)*	fair and handsome
Kent *(C)*	white or bright		

Initial sentences should be avoided when choosing a name if they could lead to embarrassment. For example:

Ulysses Fink (U. Fink)

Isidora Hirt (I. Hirt)

Alphonse Ratt (A. Ratt)

L

Laban (H)	white	Leonard (T)	brave or strong as a lion
Lachlan (C)	warlike		
Laird (C)	proprietor	Leopole (T)	patriotic
Lamar (U)	co-operative	Leroy (F)	royal
Lambert (T)	rich in land	Leslie (C)	from the gray fort
Lamont (Sc)	lawyer	Lester (AS)	from the army or camp
Lancelot (AS)	spear		
Lance		Levi (H)	a bond or promise
Landon (AS)	from the long hill	Lewis (T)	famous warrior
Landry (S)	ruler of the place	Louis	
Lane (AS)	from the country road	Lincoln (C)	from the place by the pool
Lang (T)	tall		
Lanthrop (AS)	of the village	Lindsey (OE)	from the island
Latimer (AS)	Latin teacher	Linus (H)	flax-haired
Lawrence (L)		Lionel (OF)	a young lion
Laurence		Llewellyn (C)	lightning
Lawson		Lloyd (C)	gray
Larry	victorious; crowned with laurels	Loyd	
Lars		Lorimer (L)	lover of horses
Lorenzo		Loring (T)	from Lorraine
Loren		Lot (H)	veiled
Lorenz		Lowell (AS)	beloved
Lawton (OE)	from the hillside farm	Lucas	
Leander (G)	brave; like a lion	Luke	
Lear (T)	of the meadow	Lucius (L)	light
Lee (AS)	sheltered; meadow	Lucias	
Leighton (OE)	from the meadow farm	Lucian	
		Luther (T)	renowned warrior
Leland (OE)	from the meadow land	Lyle (F)	from the island
		Lyman (OE)	man of the plains
Lemuel (H)	dedicated to God	Lyndon (OE)	of the linden tree
Leo (L)	lion	Lynn (AS)	from the waterfalls
Leon (F)		Lysander (G)	liberator

M

Macy *(U)* — enduring material
Maddock *(C)* — fire
Madison *(T)* — mighty in battle
Magnus *(L)* — great
Malcolm *(C)* — servant of St. Columbia; dove
Mallory *(OE)* — ill-omened; luckless
Malvin *(C)* } chief
Melvin
Manfred *(T)* — peach among men
Manuel — see Emmanuel
Marbie *(OE)* — from the hill by the lake
Marcus *(L)*
Mark } martial; defender
Marc
Marmaduke *(C)* — sea leader
Marsden *(AS)* — from the marsh valley
Marshall *(OF)* — marshal
Martin *(L)* } unyielding
Marty
Marvin *(T)* } famous friend or sea friend
Marwin
Mason *(L)* — stone worker
Matthew *(H)* — gift of the Lord
Maurice *(L)* } Moorish; dark
Morris
Maximilian *(L)* } the greatest
Max
Maxwell *(AS)* — dweller by the spring
Maynard *(AS)* — mightily brave
Melville *(F)* — a place
Mercer *(L)* — merchant
Meredith *(C)* } protector from the sea
Meridith
Merle *(F)* — blackbird

Merlin *(C)* } falcon; hawk
Marlen
Merrell *(T)*
Merrill } famous
Merril
Merton *(AS)* — from the place by the sea
Meyer *(T)* — farmer
Micah *(H)* — like unto the Lord
Michael *(H)* } who is like God
Mitchell
Milburn *(OE)* — from the millstream
Miles *(L)* } soldier
Myles
Milo *(L)* } miller
Millard *(OE)*
Milton *(AS)* — from the mill town
Monroe *(C)* — from the red river
Montague *(L)* — from the peaked mountain
Montgomery *(F)* — mountain hunter
Mordecai *(H)* — wise counsellor
Morgan *(W)* — dweller on the sea
Morley *(OE)* — from the moor meadow
Morrell *(L)* } swarthy
Morel
Mortimer *(F)* — ever living
Morton *(OE)* — from the moor village
Moses *(H)* — saved from the water
Murdoch *(C)* } prosperous seaman
Murdock
Murray *(C)* } seaman
Murry
Myron *(G)* } fragrant
Myreon

N

Naldo *(T)* power
Napoleon *(G)* lion from the forest
Narcissus *(G)* self-loving
Nash *(U)* alert; active
Nathan *(H)* God's gift
Nathaniel *(H)* gift of God
Neal *(C)* ⎫
Neil ⎬ a champion
Neill ⎭
Nelson *(C)* a son of Neal
Nero *(L)* black
Nestor *(G)* venerable wisdom
Neville *(L)* from the new town
Nevin *(AS)* nephew
Newlin *(C)* ⎫
Newlyn ⎬ from the new spring
Newton *(AS)* from the new estate

Nicholas *(G)* victorious among the people
Nicodemus *(G)* the people's conqueror
Nigel *(L)* dark
Noah *(H)* rest; comfort
Noel *(FL)* ⎫
Newell ⎬ Christmas
Noble *(L)* renowned; noble
Nolan *(C)* ⎫
Noland ⎬ noble or famous
Norbert *(T)* shining in the north
Norman *(OF)* ⎫
Norris ⎪
Norvin ⎬ man from the north
Norton *(AS)* ⎭
Norward *(T)* guardian of the north gate

Diminutives and Variants

Diminutives are affectionate forms that imply "little." Like big Bill and little Billy. They tend to end in *-ita, -ina, -y,* and *-ie.*

Variants are the many forms and spellings of any name. For instance, Madelon or Madie instead of the traditional Madeline.

O

Oakes *(OE)*	the oak	Ormand *(T)*	ship man
Oakley *(OE)*	from the oak tree meadow	Orson *(L)*	bear
		Orville *(F)*	lord of the manor
Obadiah *(H)*	Servant of the Lord	Osbert *(AS)*	divinely bright
Octavius *(L)*	the eighth	Osborn *(AS)*	divinely strong
Odell *(T)*	wealthy man	Oscar *(OE)*	spear of a deity
Odoric *(L)*	son of a good man	Osgood *(T)*	gift of our Lord
Ogden *(OE)*	from the oak valley	Osmond *(T)*	protected by God
Olaf *(Sc)*		Osric *(OE)*	divine ruler
Olin	} peace	Oswald *(AS)*	divine power
Olen		Otis *(G)*	keen of hearing
Oliver *(L)*	peaceful	Otto *(T)*	prosperous
Omar *(H)*	talkative	Owen *(C)*	young warrior
Ordway *(AS)*	spear fighter		
Oren *(H)*			
Orin	} pine		
Orrin			

The English-speaking world abounds with two-legged Peter Rabbits, one of whom has eleven children! There have also been infants named June Brides and June Weddings.

P

Page *(F)*	servant to the royal court	Perrin Pierce	see Peter
Paige *(U)*	helpful	Phelan *(C)*	brave as a wolf
Paine *(L)* Payne	country man or rustic	Philbert *(T)*	radiant soul
		Philip *(G)*	lover of horses
Palmer *(OE)*	palm bearer	Philo *(G)*	love
Park *(OE)* Parke Parker	keeper of the park	Phineas *(H)*	oracle
		Pierson *(OE)* Pearson	son of Peter
Parry *(F)*	guardian; protector	Pierpont *(F)* Pierrepont	dweller by the stone bridge
Pascal *(H)*	pass over		
Patrick *(L)* Padraic	noble; patrician	Pius *(L)*	pious
		Pollard *(T)*	cropped hair
Paul *(L)*	small	Porter *(L)*	doorkeeper; gate keeper
Paxton *(T)* Paxon	a traveler; from afar		
		Powell *(C)*	alert
Pembroke *(W)*	from the headland	Prentice *(L)*	apprentice; learner
Percival *(L)* Percy	piercing; a knight	Prescott *(OE)*	of the priest's dwelling
		Preston *(OE)*	of the church domain
Peregrine *(L)*	wanderer	Prince *(L)*	prince
Perry *(OE)*	the pear tree	Prior *(L)*	head of a monastery
Peter *(G)* Pedro *(Sp)* Pierre *(F)*	a rock; reliable	Proctor *(L)*	manager; leader
		Prosper *(L)*	fortunate
		Putnam *(AS)*	dweller by the pond

Q

Quartus *(L)*	the fourth son	Quincy *(L)*	from the fifth son's place
Quentin *(L)*	fifth		
Quillon *(L)*	sword	Quinn *(C)*	the wise
Quinby *(Sc)*	from woman's womb		

R

Radburn *(OE)*	} dweller by the red brook	Rene *(F)*	reborn
Radbourne		Renfred *(T)*	peacemaker
Radcliffe *(OE)*	from the red cliff	Reuben *(H)*	behold, a son!
Radford *(OE)*	dweller by the red ford	Rex *(L)*	king
		Rexford *(OE)*	from the king's ford
Radley *(OE)*	from the red field	Richard *(T)*	strong in rule
Rafael *(H)*	} God has healed	Richmond *(T)*	mighty protector
Raphael		Ridgley *(OE)*	dweller by meadow's edge
Raleigh *(OE)*	from the deer meadow		
		Riley *(T)*	valiant
Ralph *(T)*	wolf in counsel	Robert *(T)*	} bright in fame
Ralston *(OE)*	from the house of Ralph	Robin	
		Rock *(OE)*	from the rock
Ramsey *(T)*	} from the ram's island	Roderick *(T)*	famous ruler
Ramsay		Rodman *(T)*	redhead
Randolph *(T)*	} shielded or advised by wolves	Rodney *(T)*	renowned
Randal		Roger *(T)*	famous spearman
Randall		Roland *(T)*	famous land
Rawdon *(T)*	from the deer hill	Rolf	
Ray *(OF)*	kingly	Rolfe	
Rayburn *(OE)*	} from the deer brook	Rolph	} see Rudolph
Raybourne		Rollin	
Raymond *(T)*	} wise protection	Rollo	
Raymund		Romeo *(L)*	pilgrim to Rome
Reade *(OE)*	} red-haired	Romney *(L)*	a Roman
Reid		Romulus *(L)*	citizen of Rome
Reed		Ronald	see Reginald
Reece *(W)*	} enthusiastic	Rory *(C)*	ruddy; red-haired
Rhett		Roscoe *(T)*	from the deer forest
Redmond *(T)*	} adviser and protector	Ross *(T)*	horse
Redmund		Roswald *(T)*	} mighty steed
Regan *(C)*	royal; kingly	Roswell	
Reginald *(T)*	wise dominion	Roy *(L)*	king
Remus *(L)*	oarsman	Royal *(OF)*	kingly

Royce *(F)* — son of the king
Royd *(Sc)* — from the forest clearing
Royden *(OE)* — from the king's hill
Rudolph *(T)* — famous wolf
Rudyard *(U)* — tenacious

Rufus *(L)* — red-haired
Rupert — see Robert
Russell *(AS)* — like a fox; red-haired
Rutherford *(OE)* — from the cattle ford
Ryan *(U)* — capable

S

Salisbury *(OE)* — from the guarded stronghold
Salvador *(L)* — of the Savior
Samson *(H)* / Sampson — like the sun
Samuel *(H)* — name of God
Sanborn *(OE)* — from the sandy brook
Sanders *(G)* / Saunders — helper of mankind
Sandon *(OE)* — from the sandy hill
Sanford *(OE)* — from the sandy ford
Sargent *(OF)* — military attendant
Saul *(H)* — asked for
Saville *(OF)* / Savill — from the willow farm
Sawyer *(C)* — cutter of timber
Saxon *(T)* — from a Saxon town
Schuyler *(D)* — wise man; shelter
Scott *(S)* — wanderer
Seabrook *(OE)* — from the brook by the sea
Searle *(T)* / Serle / Serlo — bearing arms; wearing armor

Seaton *(OE)* / Seton — from the place by the sea
Seaver *(AS)* — victorious stronghold
Sebastian *(G)* — respected
Sedgewick *(OE)* — from the village of victory
Selby *(T)* — from the manor farm
Selwyn *(T)* — friend at the manor or palace
Seth *(H)* — the chosen or appointed
Seward *(AS)* — defender of the coast
Sewell *(T)* — victorious on the sea, mighty in victory
Seymour *(T)* — famed at sea
Shaw *(OE)* — from the shady grove
Shelby *(AS)* — from the ledge farm
Sheldon *(AS)* — from the hill-ledge
Shelley *(AS)* — from the ledge meadow
Shepard *(AS)* / Shepherd / Sheppard — sheep tender
Shepley *(AS)* — of the sheep meadow

Sherard *(AS)*	valiant soldier	Stacey *(L)*	stable; dependable
Sheridan *(C)*	wild man	Stacy	
Sherlock *(OE)*	fair haired son	Stafford *(OE)*	from the landing ford
Sherman *(AS)*	wool-shearer or cutter	Standish *(OE)*	from the stony park
Sherwin *(AS)*	a true friend	Stanfield *(OE)*	from the stony field
Sherwood *(OE)*	from the bright forest	Stanford	
Sibley *(AS)*	friendly	Stanhope *(OE)*	from the stony hollow
Sidney *(F)*	follower of St. Denis	Stanislaus *(Sl)*	glory of the camp
Sydney		Stanley *(OE)*	dweller by the stony sea
Simpson	see Samson		
Siegfried *(T)*	victorious peace	Stanton *(AS)*	from the stone dwelling
Sigmund *(T)*	victorious protection		
Silas *(L)*		Stanway *(OE)*	dweller by the stone highway
Silvanus	of the woods		
Sylvanus		Stanwood *(OE)*	from the stony wood
Silvester		Stephen *(G)*	crown
Sylvester		Steven	
Simeon *(H)*	servant of the Lord	Sterling *(T)*	good value; genuine
Simon *(H)*	obedient	Stirling	
Sinclair *(L)*	illustrious	Stewart *(AS)*	keeper of the estate
Sion *(H)*	exalted	Stuart	
Sloan *(C)*	warrior	Stillman *(AS)*	quiet; gentle
Sloane		Stillwell *(AS)*	from the still spring
Sol *(L)*	the sun	Stoddard *(OE)*	keeper of horses
Solomon *(H)*	peaceable	Sumner *(OF)*	summoner
Spencer *(OE)*	storekeeper; dispenser of provisions	Sutton *(OE)*	from the south village or town
Spenser			
Sprague *(OE)*	alert; quick	Swaine *(T)*	boy

John and Mary, in all their forms, are the two all–time favorite first names.

John has over ninety variants including Evan (Welsh), Giovanni (Italian), Hans (Dutch), Ivan (Russian), Jens (Danish), Sean (Irish), Jan (Polish), Juan (Spanish), and Jean (French), as well as the familiar Jack, Johnny and Jock.

Other forms of Mary include Polly, Molly, Marion, Marie, Maureen, Maria, Mitzi, Mamie and Manon, as in the opera.

T

Taber *(OF)* — herald

Tait *(T)* }
Tate — cheerful

Talbott *(AS)* — bloodhound
Tavis *(C)* — son of David
Taylor *(L)* — a tailor
Teague *(C)* — poet
Tearle *(OE)* — stem

Tedman *(T)* }
Tedmund — protector of the nation

Tedric — from Derek

Terence *(L)* }
Terrence — tender

Terrill *(T)* — martial; belonging to Thor

Tertius *(L)* — the third
Thaddeus *(H)* — praise to God

Thatcher *(AS)* }
Thacher — mender of roofs
Thaxter }

Thayer *(T)* — of the nation's army
Theodore *(G)* — gift of God
Theodric *(T)* — the people's ruler
Theron *(G)* — hunter
Thomas *(H)* — the twin; good company

Thor *(Sc)* — thunderous one
Thornton *(AS)* — from the thorn tree place

Thorpe *(AS)* — from the small village
Thurlow *(Sc)* — from Thor's mountain
Thurman *(Sc)* — under Thor's protection

Thurston *(Sc)* — Thor's stone
Tilden *(OE)* — from the fertile valley
Tilford *(OE)* — from the fertile ford
Timothy *(G)* — revering God
Tirrell — see Terrill
Titus *(L)* — saved

Tobias *(H)* }
Tobin — God's goodness

Todd *(L)* — the fox
Toland *(AS)* — from the taxed land
Tolman *(AS)* — collector of taxes
Torrance — see Terence
Torrey *(C)* — dweller by the forest
Townsend *(AS)* — from the end of the town

Tracey *(AS)* }
Tracy — brave defender

Trahern *(C)* — stronger than iron

Travers *(OFL)* }
Travis — from the crossroad

Tramayne *(C)* }
Tremain — from the town of the stone

Trent *(L)* — swift
Trevor *(C)* — prudent traveler
Trey *(ME)* — three

Tristram *(L)* }
Tristan — sorrowful

Truman *(AS)* — a faithful man
Tudor *(G)* — divine gift
Turner *(L)* — worker with the lathe
Tybalt *(T)* — leader of the people
Tyler *(OE)* — maker of tiles
Tyson *(T)* — son of the German

U

Udo *(U)* — sacrifices personal comfort for general good
Uland *(T)* — from the noble land
Ulric *(T)*
Ulrick — } ruler of all
Ulysses *(L)* — venturer

Unni *(H)* — modest
Upton *(AS)* — from the high town
Urban *(L)* — from the city; sophisticated
Uriah *(H)* — the Lord is my light
Urian *(G)* — from heaven
Uziel *(H)* — a mighty force

V

Vachel *(F)* — keeper of the cattle
Valdis *(T)* — spirited in battle
Vale *(FL)*
Vail — } from the valley
Valentine *(L)* — healthy; strong; valorous
Valerian *(L)* — strong
Vance *(T)* — son of a famous family
Vandyke *(T)* — of the dyke
Van Ness *(T)* — of the headland
Varden *(FC)*
Vardon — } from the green hill

Varian *(L)* — clever; capricious
Vaughan *(C)*
Vaughn — } small or little
Vere *(L)* — true
Vernon *(L)* — flourishing
Victor *(L)* — conqueror
Vincent *(L)* — conquering one
Vinson *(AS)* — son of Vinn
Virgil *(L)* — strong; flourishing
Vito *(L)* — vital
Vivien *(L)* — lively
Vladimir *(Sl)* — world ruler
Volney *(T)* — most popular

W

Wade *(AS)* wanderer
Wadsworth
(OE) from Wade's castle
Walcott *(OE)* ⎫ dweller in the walled
Walcot ⎭ cottage
Waldemar *(T)* strong and famous
Waldon *(OE)* from the wooded hill
Waldron *(T)* mighty raven
Walker *(OE)* forester
Wallace *(T)* foreigner
Walter *(T)* powerful; of great
destiny
Walton *(OE)* from the enclosed
farmstead
Ward *(AS)* guardian
Ware *(AS)* careful; prudent
Warfield *(OE)* from the field by the
dam
Waring *(AS)* cautious
Warner *(T)* protecting warrior
Warren *(T)* protecting friend
Warwick *(T)* ⎫
Warrick ⎭ strong ruler
Warton *(OE)* from the poplar-tree
farm
Washburn *(U)* regard for convention
Washington purifying
(Sa)
Watson *(AS)* warrior's son
Wayland *(OE)* from the land by the
highway
Wayne *(OE)* wagon-maker
Webster *(OE)* weaver
Welby *(OE)* from the farm by the
spring

Weldon *(OE)* from the spring by
the hill
Wellington *(AS)* from the prosperous
estate
Wells *(OE)* dweller by the spring
Wendell *(T)* ⎫
Wendel ⎭ wanderer
Wescott *(AS)* dwells at the west
cottage
Wesley *(AS)* ⎫
Wellesley ⎬ from the west
Westley ⎭ meadow
Weston *(OE)* from the west village
Weylin *(C)* son of the wolf
Whitby *(AS)* from the white
dwellings
Whitelaw *(AS)* of the white hill
Whitney *(AS)* from the white island
Wilburn *(AS)* inventive
Wiatt see Wyatt
Wilber see Wilburn
Wildon *(OE)* from the wooded hill
Wilfred *(T)* ⎫
Wilfrid ⎭ desired peace
Willard *(Sa)* protecting
William *(T)* determined protector
Willis *(T)* son of William
Wilmer *(T)* ⎫
Wilmar ⎭ beloved and famous
Wilmot *(T)* beloved heart
Wilson *(T)* son of William
Wilton *(OE)* from the farmstead by
the spring
Winchell *(AS)* drawer of water
Winfield *(AS)* from the friendly field

Windsor *(T)*	at the bend of the river	Woodrow *(OE)*	from the hedgerow by the forest
Winsor			
Winfred *(T)*	joyous peace	Woodward *(OE)*	keeper of the forest
Winfrid			
Winslow *(AS)*	friendly	Worden *(OE)*	guardian
Winston *(AS)*	from the friendly town	Worthington *(AS)*	from the riverside
Winthrop *(AS)*	from the friendly village	Wright *(OE)*	craftsman
		Wyatt *(OE)*	guide
Wirt *(AS)*	worthy	Wylie *(AS)*	beguiling
Wolfe *(T)*	wolf	Wyman *(AS)*	warrior
Wolfram *(T)*	respected; feared	Wyndham *(OE)*	from the windy village
Wolfgang *(T)*	path of a wolf		
Woodley *(OE)*	from the wooded meadow	Wynne *(U)*	intuitive; sympathetic

X

Xavier *(A)*	brilliant	Xerxes *(P)*	king
Xenos *(G)*	stronger		

Saint Regis Paper Company reduced its percentage of defective bags from six to one when it began putting each machine operator's name, rather than number, on each bag.

Y

Yale *(T)*	payer	Yates *(OE)*	dweller by the gates
Yancy *(F)*	Englishman	York *(L)*	sacred tree
Yardley *(OE)*	from the enclosed meadow	Yves *(F)*	an archer

Z

Zaccheus *(H)*	pure	Zebedee *(H)*	a blessing
Zachariah *(H)*		Zebulon *(H)*	dwelling place
Zacharias	God has remembered	Zelig *(T)*	blessed
Zachary		Zenas *(G)*	gift of Zeus
Zane *(U)*	form of John	Zephaniah *(H)*	the Lord has hidden
Zebadiah *(H)*	the Lord's gift		

The Very Best Names
For Baby Girls

Key to abbreviations used in the following pages

American Indian *(Am.Ind.)*
Anglo-Saxon *(AS)*
Arabic *(A)*
Aramaean *(Ar)*
Celtic *(C)*
Danish *(Da)*
Egyptian *(Eg)*
English *(E)*
French *(F)*
French-Celtic *(FC)*
French-Latin *(FL)*
Gaelic *(Ga)*
Greek *(G)*
Hebrew *(H)*
Hebrew-Latin *(HL)*
Italian *(It)*
Japanese*(J)*
Latin *(L)*
Middle English *(ME)*

Norse *(N)*
Old English *(OE)*
Old French *(OF)*
Old French Latin*(OFL)*
Persian *(P)*
Russian*(Russ)*
Sanskrit *(San)*
Saxon *(Sa)*
Scandinavian *(Sc)*
Slavonic *(Sl)*
Spanish *(Sp)*
Spanish-Arabic *(SpA)*
Spanish-Latin *(SpL)*
Swiss *(Sw)*
Teutonic *(T)*
Teutonic-Latin *(TL)*
Uncertain *(U)*
Welsh *(W)*

A

Abigail *(H)* — source of joy
Ada *(H)* — joyous
Adabel *(T)*
Adabelle — happy and fair
Adah *(H)* — ornament
Adalia *(T)* — noble
Adela *(T)*
Adelaide
Adele — of noble rank
Adiel *(H)* — ornament of the Lord
Adine *(H)*
Adina — delicate
Adna *(H)* — pleasure
Adora *(T)* — the beloved
Adria *(L)* — the unknown
Adrienne *(L)* — woman of the sea
Agatha *(G)* — good
Agnes *(G)* — pure, chaste
Aida — see Ada
Aileen *(G)* — light
Ailsa *(T)* — of good cheer
Aimee *(F)* — beloved
Airlia *(G)* — ethereal
Alana *(C)*
Alanna — fair, comely
Alarice *(T)* — ruler of all
Alberta *(T)* — noble and brilliant
Alda *(T)* — rich
Aldercy *(OE)* — chief or prince
Aldis *(OE)*
Aldys — from the house
Aldora *(G)* — winged gift
Alethea *(G)* — picturesque
Alexandra *(G)*
Alexis — helper of mankind

Alfreda *(T)* — supernaturally wise
Alice *(T)*
Alicia
Alison
Allis — noble
Alyse
Allison
Alida *(G)* — from the city of fine vestments
Allegra *(L)* — cheerful
Alma *(L)* — cherishing
Almira *(A)* — princess
Alodie *(AS)* — wealthy, prosperous
Aloyse *(T)*
Aloysia — famous in battle
Alta *(L)* — high
Althea *(G)* — wholesome, healing
Alva *(L)* — white
Alvina *(T)* — beloved; friend of all
Alvita *(L)* — vivacious
Alysia *(G)* — captivating
Alyssa *(T)* — noble; of good cheer
Amabel *(L)* — lovable
Amanda *(L)* — worthy to be loved
Amara *(G)* — unfading
Amaris *(H)* — whom God has promised
Amaryllis *(G)* — fresh, sparkling
Amber *(A)* — a jewel
Amelia *(T)* — industrious
Amena *(C)* — honest
Amethyst *(G)* — sober
Amity *(L)* — friendly
Amorette *(L)* — little love; sweetheart
Amy *(L)* — beloved

Anastasia *(G)*	one who will rise again	Ardis *(L)*	} fervent; eager
Anatola *(G)*	of the east	Ardra	
Andrea *(It)*	womanly	Aretina *(G)*	virtuous
Angela *(G)*	} angel; heavenly messenger	Ariadne *(G)*	holy one
Angelica		Ariana *(W)*	silvery
Angelina		Arlene *(C)*	} a pledge
Anita *(Sp)*		Arleen	
Ann *(H)*		Arlana	
Anna	} full of grace	Ariella *(H)*	ethereal
Anne		Astra *(G)*	like a star
Annette		Astrid *(Sc)*	beautiful as a goddess
Anselma *(T)*	protectress	Atalaya *(SpA)*	a watch tower
Anthea *(G)*	like a flower	Atalie *(Sw)*	pure
Antonia *(L)*	super excellent; incomparable	Athena *(G)*	wisdom
		Audrey *(OE)*	noble strength
Antoinette *(F)*	see Antonia	Audris *(T)*	fortunate
Aphrodite *(G)*	goddess of love	Augusta *(L)*	majestic, exalted
April *(L)*	to open	Aurelia *(L)*	golden
Arabella *(L)*	fair and beautiful	Avis *(L)*	} a bird
Araminta *(H)*	lofty	Ava	
Ardath *(AS)*	} rich gift	Azalia *(H)*	whom the Lord has spared
Ardith			

The Fashions in Name Game

Mary was "it" before the fashions came.
Now Jennifer's the grand "new" name.
With Tiffany climbing, who knows who'll be
Tops at the turn of the century.
　　　　Barbara Shook Hazen

B

Babette *(F)*	dim. of Elizabeth	Bettina	
Barbara *(G)*	mysterious; foreign	Betty	see Elizabeth
Bathsheba *(H)*	daughter of our oath	Beth	
Beata *(L)*	blessed	Beulah *(H)*	married
Beatrice *(L)*	she brings joy	Beverly *(AS)*	beaver meadow
Belinda *(E)*	shining, bright	Blanche *(OF)*	
Belle *(F)*	beautiful	Bianca	white; fair
Bena *(H)*	wise	Blenda *(T)*	dazzling, glorious
Benita *(L)*		Blythe *(AS)*	happy, joyous
Benedicata	the blessed	Bonnie *(OE)*	pretty, sweet
Bernardine *(T)*		Bonita *(Sp)*	pretty
Bernardette	brave; strong	Brenda *(T)*	fiery
Bernice *(G)*	bringing victory	Brenna *(C)*	maiden with raven
Bertha *(T)*	bright		hair
Bertilde *(T)*	commanding	Briana *(C)*	the strong
Beryl *(H)*	jewel	Bridget *(C)*	
Bess		Bridgette	strong
Bessie		Brooke *(E)*	from the brook
Betsy	see Elizabeth	Brunhilde *(T)*	battle heroine
Bette			

C

Calandra *(G)*	the lark	Carin *(L)*	
Camilla *(L)*		Caryn	the keel
Camille	noble, self-sacrificing	Carina	
Candace *(L)*		Carla *(T)*	one who is strong
Candida	pure, glowing	Carlene	
Candice		Carleen	see Caroline
Cara *(C)*	friend	Carlin	

Carlotta *(Sp)*	noble birth	Christa *(G)*	Christian
Carmel *(H)*	garden land	Christine *(G)*	fair Christian
Carmen *(L)*	song	Chrystal *(E)*	glass
Carol *(OF)*	song of joy	Clara *(L)*	
Caroline *(T)*		Claire	bright; clear
Carolyn	one who is strong	Clarabelle *(L)*	bright, shining
Carrie		Clarissa *(L)*	
Cary *(C)*	dark of hair or	Clarice	making famous
Carey	complexion	Claudia *(L)*	
Cassandra *(G)*	prophetess	Claudette	dazzling
Catharine		Clematis *(G)*	clinging
Catherine	see Katherine	Clementine *(L)*	kind, merciful
Cathleen		Cleopatra *(G)*	
Cecilia *(L)*		Cleo	famous
Cecile		Clotilde *(T)*	
Cecily	musical	Clothilda	famous battle maiden
Celia		Clyte *(G)*	a nymph
Celeste *(L)*		Colette *(G)*	
Celesta	heavenly	Collette	victorious
Celestine		Colleen *(Ga)*	girl
Chandra *(San)*	she outshines the stars	Constance *(L)*	unchanging; loyal
Charissa *(G)*	graceful	Consuela *(L)*	consolation
Charity *(L)*	charitable, loving	Cora *(G)*	
Charlotte *(T)*		Corinne	maiden
Charlene	strong; noble-spirited	Cordelia *(L)*	sincere
Charmaine *(L)*	little song	Cornelia *(L)*	womanly virtue
Cherie *(F)*		Crystal *(G)*	pure
Cheryl	dear one	Cynthia *(G)*	moon goddess
Chloe *(G)*	blossoming		

Alliterative names are nice to say
like Calvin Coolidge and Dolores Darsay.

D

Dagmar *(Da)*	joy of the land
Daisy *(E)*	daisy
Dale *(T)*	dweller in the valley
Dama *(L)*	lady
Damara *(G)*	gentle girl
Danielle *(H)*	God has judged
Daphne *(G)*	laurel
Dara *(H)*	the heart of wisdom
Darcie *(FC)* Darcey	from the stronghold
Darda *(H)*	pearl of wisdom
Darice *(P)*	queenly
Darlene *(AS)* Darleen Darline	dearly beloved
Daryl *(OE)*	beloved, dear
Davina *(H)*	loved one
Dawn *(AS)*	break of day
Deanna	see Diana
Deborah *(H)*	industrious
Decima *(L)*	the tenth
Dierdre *(Ga)*	sorrowful
Delia *(G)* Della	from Delos
Delilah *(H)*	temptress; coquette
Delora *(L)* Delores	from the seashore
Delphine *(G)*	calm; serene
Demetria *(G)*	from the fertile land
Denise *(G)* Denys	worshipper
Desdemona *(G)*	girl of sadness
Desiree *(FL)*	hoped-for
Desma *(G)*	pledge or bond
Devona *(AS)*	the defender
Diana *(L)* Diane	moon goddess; perfect
Dinah *(H)* Dina	judgment
Dione *(G)*	daughter of heaven and earth
Dolores *(L)*	Our Lady of Sorrows
Dominica *(L)* Dominique	born on the Lord's day
Donella *(L)*	little mistress
Donna *(L)*	lady
Dora *(G)*	gift
Dorcas *(G)*	gazelle
Dorinda *(G)*	bountiful gift
Doris *(G)* Doria	sea goddess
Dorothy *(G)* Dorothea	God's gift
Drusilla *(G)*	soft-eyed
Dulcie *(L)*	sweet, charming

E

Echo *(G)*   a Greek nymph
Edana *(C)*   fiery; ardent
Eden *(H)*   delightful; enchanting
Edith *(T)* ⎫
Editha ⎬ rich gift; stately
Edlyn *(AS)*   of the nobility
Edna *(G)*   delight
Edwina *(AS)*   valued friend
Effie *(G)*   fair and famed
Eileen   see Aileen
Elaine *(G)*   light; bright
Elberta   see Alberta
Eleanor *(G)* ⎫
Eleanora ⎬ light
Elena ⎫
Elinor ⎪
Ella ⎬ see Helen
Ellen ⎭
Electra *(G)*   shining star
Elfreda *(T)*   noble and wise
Elizabeth *(H)* ⎫
Elisabeth ⎪
Else ⎪
Elsia ⎪
Elsie ⎬ consecrated to God
Elise ⎪
Eliza ⎪
Elsbeth ⎭
Elma *(G)*   pleasant
Eloise *(OF)*   romantic

Elva *(T)*   elf
Elvira *(Sp)*   like an elf
Emily *(T)* ⎫
Emilia ⎬ industrious
Emma *(T)*   one who heals
Emmeline *(E)*   intellectual
Endora *(H)*   fountain
Enid *(C)*   quiet; pure
Erica *(Sc)*   of royalty
Erin ⎫
Erina *(C)* ⎬ girl from Ireland
Ernestine *(T)*   purposeful; earnest
Esmerelda *(G)*   emerald
Estelle *(L)*   a star
Esther *(H)*   a star
Ethel *(T)*   noble
Eudora *(G)*   wonderful or
    delightful gift
Eugenia *(G)*   well-born
Eunice *(G)*   bringing a happy
    victory
Euphemia *(G)*   accomplished; famed
Eurydice *(G)*   broad separation
Evadne *(G)*   fortunate; faithful
Evangeline *(G)*   bearer of good news
Eve *(H)* ⎫
Eva ⎪
Evelyn ⎬ life
Evita ⎭

Giving a name, indeed, is a poetic art.
Thomas Carlyle

F

Faith (L)	
Faye	faithful
Fay	
Fanchon (T)	free
Farrah (ME)	beautiful
Faustine (T)	lucky
Felice (L)	
Felicia	
Felise	happiness
Felicite	
Fern (G)	feather
Fidela (L)	
Fidelia	faithful
Fifi	see Josephine
Fiona (C)	
Fionna	ivory-skinned

Flavia (L)	blond
Fleur (F)	a flower
Fleurette (F)	little flower
Flora (L)	goddess of flowers
Florence (L)	blooming; flourishing
Fonda (SpL)	profound
Frances (T)	
Francesca	free
Francine	
Freda (T)	
Freida	peace
Frieda	
Fredericka (T)	peaceful
Fritzie (T)	
Fritzi	peaceful ruler

G

Gail	
Gayle	see Abigail
Gale	
Gabrielle (H)	woman of God
Garnet (T)	radiant red jewel
Gay (F)	merry
Gemini (G)	
Gemima	twin
Georgiana (G)	
Georgia	earth-lover
Georgette	

Geraldine (T)	affectionate
Gerda (T)	the protected
Germaine (F)	exquisite
Gertrude (T)	strength of a spear
Gilberta (T)	bright pledge
Gilda (C)	God's servant
Giselle (T)	
Gisela	pledge or promise
Gittel (H)	maiden of the winepress
Gladys (W)	demure; delicate

Glenna *(Ga)*
Glenda   } from the glen
Glynis
Gloria *(L)*   glorious
Grace *(L)*   favor; grace
Greer *(G)*   watchwoman
Greta   } see Margaret
Gretchen

Griselda *(T)*   heroine
Guinevere *(C)*   fair lady
Gwendolyn *(C)*
Gwendolen   } white-browed; fair
Gwynne

H

Hagar *(H)*   flight
Hannah *(H)*   grace; compassion
Harriet *(T)*
Harrietta   } mistress of the home
Hatty
Hazel *(AS)*   authority
Heartha *(T)*   earth mother
Heather *(AS)*   the heather
Hedda *(T)*   war
Hedwig *(T)*   storm; strife
Helen *(G)*
Helena   } light
Helga *(T)*   holy
Helsa *(H)*   given to God
Henrietta *(T)*   rule of the house

Hephzibah *(H)*   my joy is in her
Hera *(G)*   Greek Queen of the Gods
Hermione *(G)*   of the earth
Hermosa *(S)*   beautiful
Hesper *(G)*   evening star
Hester *(P)*   a star
Hilary *(L)*   cheerful
Heloise   see Louise
Hilda *(T)*
Hildegarde   } strong
Holly *(AS)*   the holly
Honora *(L)*   honorable
Hope *(AS)*   hope
Hortense *(L)*   garden worker

The eureka! feeling: when the name suddenly hits and you know this is "it."

I

Ianthe *(G)*	delightful	Iona *(G)*	purple jewel
Ida *(T)*	} happy	Irene *(G)*	peace
Idette		Iris *(G)*	a rainbow
Idelia *(T)*	noble	Irma *(T)*	strong
Idola *(G)*	vision	Isabel	
Idona *(T)*	industrious	Isabelle	} see Elizabeth
Ignacia *(L)*	ardent	Isobel	
Ilka *(TL)*	hard worker	Isadora *(G)*	a gift
Imogene *(L)*	image	Isolde *(C)*	fair
Ina *(G)*	pure	Ivah *(H)*	
Inez *(Sp)*	chaste	Ivana	} God's gracious gift
Inga *(Sc)*	} a daughter	Ivy *(OE)*	from the ivy tree
Ingrid			

J

Jacinta *(G)*	beautiful; comely	Jessica *(H)*	grace of God
Jacqueline *(H)*	the supplanter	Jewel *(OF)*	precious
Jada *(H)*	} wise	Joan *(H)*	
Jadda		Joann	
Jamila *(M)*	beautiful	Joanna	} God's gracious gift
Jane *(H)*		Johanna	
Janet		Jobina *(H)*	the afflicted
Janice	} God's grace	Jocelyn *(L)*	fair; merry
Jayne		Joleen *(ME)*	} He will increase
Jenny		Jolene	
Jean	} see Joan	Josephine *(H)*	she shall add
Jeannette		Joy *(OF)*	delight
Jennifer *(C)*	white wave	Joyce *(OF)*	joyful

Judith *(H)*			Juliet	
Jodi	} praise of the Lord		Jill	} youthful
Judy			June *(L)*	young
Julia *(L)*			Justine *(L)*	
Juliana	} youthful		Justa	} the just

K

Kara		Kendra *(AS)*	the knowing woman
Karen		Kerry *(G)*	dark one
Karin		Kimberly *(OE)*	from the royal fortress
Katherine *(G)*			meadow
Katharine	} pure	Kira *(P)*	the sun
Kathryn		Kirby *(AS)*	from the church town
Kaitlin		Kirsten *(Sc)*	the anointed one
Katrina		Koren *(G)*	young girl
Kitty		Kristin *(Sc)*	Christian
Kay *(G)*	rejoicing	Kyla *(Ga)*	comely
Kelly *(Ga)*	warrior maid		

Yes, Virginia, there really have been real children named for the whole alphabet, as was "Pat" from Michigan whose birth certificate read Althea Beverly Carol Diana Eva Felice Greta Harline Io Joanne Karen Laquite Maurine Naomi Orpha Patricia Queenie Rebecca Shirley Teresa Una Valeeta Wanda Xelia Yolanda Zoe.

L

Lalita *(San)*	artless	Lillian *(L)*	
Lana *(C)*	handsome	Lila	
Lara *(L)*	well-known	Lilian	} pure as a lily
Laura *(L)*		Lilyan	
Laurel		Lillith *(H)*	evil woman
Lauren		Lily	} see Lillian
Laureen	} the laurel; famous	Lilybelle	
Lora		Linda *(Sp)*	beautiful
Loretta		Lisa *(H)*	} consecrated to God
Lorna		Liza	
Laverne *(F)*	springlike	Lois	see Louise
Lavinia *(L)*	woman of Rome	Lola	see Charlotte
Leah *(H)*	} the weary	Lorelei *(T)*	temptress
Lea		Lorraine *(T)*	famous in battle
Lee *(AS)*	meadow	Lotus *(Eg)*	bloom of
Leila *(Ar)*	black, dark as night		forgetfulness
Lenore	see Helen	Louise *(T)*	romantic
Leona *(L)*	} the lion	Lucy *(T)*	light
Leonie		Lucille	
Leontine *(L)*	} brave as a lion	Lucia	} see Lucy
Leora		Lucinda	
Leslie *(C)*	} from the gray fort	Luella *(L)*	the appeaser
Lesley		Luna *(L)*	the moon
Leta *(L)*	} joy; delight	Lydia *(G)*	intelligent
Letitia		Lynn	
Libby *(H)*	consecrated to God	Lynne *(AS)*	} cascade
Lida *(Sl)*	} loved by all	Lynna	
Lyda		Lyris *(G)*	lyrical

Futuristic Thought: The name you find in the baby-naming book may be the name later arrivals find in the history books.

M

Mabel *(L)*	} lovable	Mathilda *(T)*	} courageous	
Maybelle		Maude		
Madeline *(H)*	} tower of strength	Matilda *(G)*	brave in battle	
Madeleine		Maureen *(L)*	} dark	
Madelyn		Maurita		
Madra *(L)*	mother	Mavis *(C)*	songbird	
Mae *(ME)*	} maiden	Maxine *(L)*	the greatest	
May		Medea *(G)*	part goddess	
Magda	see Madeleine	Megan *(C)*	} the strong	
Maida *(AS)*	maiden	Meghan		
Malina *(H)*	from a high tower	Mehetable *(H)*	one of God's favored	
Mamie	see Mary	Melanie *(G)*	blackness	
Mara	see Mary	Melinda *(Sa)*	grateful	
Marcella *(L)*	} of Mars	Melissa *(G)*	honey bee	
Marcia		Melodie *(G)*	song	
Margaret *(G)*	⎫	Melvina *(C)*	chief	
Margery		Mercedes *(Sp)*	merciful	
Margot	} a pearl	Meredith *(C)*	protector of the sea	
Marjorie		Merle *(L)*	} blackbird	
Marquerite		Meryl		
Marian		Merritt *(AS)*	of merit	
Marie		Meta *(L)*	ambitious	
Marion	} see Mary	Mia *(L)*	mine	
Marietta		Michele *(F)*	} who is like God	
Marilyn	⎭	Michelle		
Marina *(L)*	sea maiden	Mignon *(OF)*	dainty	
Maris *(L)*	see star	Mildred *(OF)*	gentle strength	
Marleen	} see Madeline	Millicent *(T)*	strength	
Marlene		Mimi *(T)*	resolute opponent	
Marsha	see Marcia	Minerva *(G)*	} wise	
Martha *(Ar)*	} the lady	Minni		
Marta		Minna *(T)*	loving memory	
Martina *(L)*	belonging to Mars	Mirabel *(L)*	of great beauty	
Mary *(H)*	} bitter; sympathetic	Miranda *(L)*	to be admired	
Marie		Miriam *(H)*	see Mary	

Mitzie	see Margaret	Morla *(H)*	chosen by the Lord
Modesta *(L)*	shy	Morna *(Ga)*	tender and gentle
Moira	see Mary	Moya *(C)*	the great
Mollie		Muriel *(H)*	bittersweet
Mona *(Ga)*	solidarity	Myra *(L)*	wonderful
Monica *(L)*	advisor	Myrtle *(G)*	victorious crown

N

Nadine *(F)*	} hope	Nerissa *(G)*	of the sea
Nada		Nicole *(G)*	} victory of the people
Nan	} see Ann	Nicolette	
Nancy		Nichola	
Nanette		Niobe *(G)*	tearful
Nanna *(H)*	} grace	Noel *(L)*	Christmas child
Nana		Nola *(C)*	noble; famous
Naomi *(H)*	pleasant	Nona *(L)*	the ninth
Narda *(P)*	anointed	Nora	} see Eleanor, Helen
Natalie *(L)*	} child of Christmas	Norah	
Nathalie		Noreen	see Honora
Natasha		Norma *(L)*	model
Neda *(Sl)*	Sunday's child	Nydia *(L)*	a refuge
Nelda *(OE)*	of the elder tree	Nyssa *(G)*	} starting point
Nerine *(G)*	sea nymph	Nissa	

Choice Thought: Choose a name you like to say. If baby's name is written or said even ten times a day, that makes 292,000 times by the time "baby" is eighty!

O

Octavia *(L)*	the eighth one	Ondine *(H)*	wave
Odele *(G)*	melody	Opal *(San)*	jewel
Odelia *(T)*	prosperous	Ophelia *(G)*	wise
Odette *(F)*	home lover	Oriana *(L)*	golden
Ola *(Sc)*	daughter or descendant	Oribel *(L)*	golden beauty
		Oriole *(L)*	golden thrush
Olga *(T)*	holy	Oriel	
Olivia *(L)*	olive; peace-bringer	Orlena *(L)*	golden
Olive		Orna *(I)*	olive-colored
Olympia *(G)*	of the mountain of the Gods	Ottilie *(T)*	battle heroine

Actress Tuesday Weld was originally named Thursday for the day of the week on which she was born. Her mother later decided Thursday looked more like a Tuesday and began calling her that.

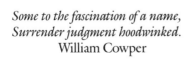

Some to the fascination of a name,
Surrender judgment hoodwinked.
William Cowper

P

Paige *(AS)*	young; child
Page	
Paloma *(Sp)*	dove
Pamela *(G)*	honey; loving
Pandora *(G)*	gifted
Pansy *(F)*	thought
Patience *(L)*	patient
Patricia *(L)*	of the nobility; well-born
Patty	
Patsy	
Paula *(L)*	little
Paulette	
Pauline	
Pearl *(E)*	pearl
Pegeen *(C)*	
Penelope *(G)*	weaver; industrious
Peony *(G)*	flower
Pepita *(Sp)*	she shall add
Perdita *(L)*	lost
Persephone *(G)*	weaver of dreams
Persis	

Petra *(G)*	rock
Petrina *(G)*	steadfast
Petula *(OF)*	peevish
Petulah	
Phenice *(H)*	from a palm tree
Philana *(G)*	friend of mankind
Philippa *(G)*	lover of horses
Philomena *(G)*	loving friend
Pheobe *(G)*	shining
Phyllis *(G)*	green leaf
Pia *(L)*	devout
Polly	see Mary
Pomona *(L)*	fragrant
Poppy *(U)*	from the poppy
Portia *(L)*	doorway
Prima *(L)*	first born
Primrose *(L)*	first rose
Priscilla *(L)*	of long lineage
Prudence *(L)*	prudent
Psyche *(G)*	soul

Q

Queena *(OE)*	woman; queen
Quenby *(Sc)*	wife; womanly
Querida *(Sp)*	loved one

Questa *(L)*	seeker
Quinta *(L)*	fifth child
Quirita *(L)*	citizen

R

Rachel *(H)*		Roberta *(AS)*	
Rae	} motherly	Robin	} of shining fame
Ray		Roderica *(T)*	princess
Ramona *(T)*	protector	Rolanda *(T)*	famous
Rana *(San)*	} royal	Roma *(L)*	woman of Rome
Raina		Ronalda *(T)*	powerful
Raphaela *(H)*	blessed healer	Rosabel *(L)*	beautiful rose
Rebba *(H)*	fourth child	Rosalie *(L)*	festival of roses
Rebecca *(H)*	} tie; bond	Rosalind *(L)*	} fair rose
Reba		Roslyn	
Regina *(L)*	queenly	Rosanne *(L)*	gracious rose
Renata	} see Irene	Rose *(L)*	
Rene		Rosa	} rose
Renita *(L)*	poised; firm	Rosamond	
Renee *(F)*	reborn	Rosemarie *(L)*	Mary's rose
Rhea *(G)*	motherly	Rowena *(C)*	flowing fair hair
Rhoda *(G)*	rose	Roxana *(P)*	} dawn
Rita *(G)*	pearl	Roxanne	
Riva *(OF)*	dreamer	Ruby *(OF)*	red
Roanna *(L)*	sweet; gracious	Ruth *(H)*	friend

S

Sabrina *(AS)*	a princess	Samara *(H)*	watchful; cautious
Sacha *(G)*	helpmate	Samuela *(H)*	} name of God
Sadie	} see Sarah	Samantha	
Sallie		Sandra *(G)*	helper of mankind
Salena *(G)*	salty	Sarah *(H)*	princess
Salome *(H)*	woman of perfection	Selena *(G)*	moon-goddess

Selma *(C)*	fair	Stella *(L)*	star
Seraphine *(H)*	deeply religious	Stephanie *(G)*	crown
Serena *(L)*	tranquil	Stephenie	
Sharon *(H)*	of the land of Sharon	Susan *(H)*	
Sheila *(C)*	musical	Susanna	lily
Sherri	see Sarah	Susanne	
Sherry		Suzette	
Shirley *(AS)*	from the white meadow	Sybil *(G)*	prophetess
		Sydel *(H)*	enchantress
Simone *(H)*	heard by the Lord	Sydney *(H)*	the enticer
Sophia *(G)*	wisdom	Sylvia *(L)*	forest maiden
Sonia		Silvia	
Sonya			

T

Tabitha *(Ar)*	a gazelle	Thoela *(G)*	heaven-sent
Tallulah *(Am. Ind.)*	leaping water	Thera *(G)*	untamed
		Thomasina *(H)*	the twin
Tamara *(H)*	the palm tree	Thora *(T)*	thunder
Tammy		Tiffany *(F)*	sheer silk or cotton
Tania *(Russ)*	fairy queen	Timothea *(G)*	honoring God
Tanya		Tina	short form of all names ending in "tina"
Tansy *(G)*	persistent		
Tara *(C)*	tower		
Teresa *(G)*	harvester; reaper	Tobey *(H)*	God is good
Theresa		Tonia *(L)*	beyond praise
Therese		Tory	short form of Victoria
Tessa *(G)*	fourth	Tracy *(G)*	brave battler
Thalia *(G)*	abundance	Tracey	
Thea *(G)*	goddess	Trista *(L)*	sorrowful
Thelma *(G)*	nurse	Trixie	see Beatrice
Theodora *(G)*	Divine gift	Trudy *(G)*	beloved
Theodosia		Tuesday *(OE)*	Tuesday
Theda			
Theo			

U

Udele *(OE)*	woman of great wealth
Ula *(C)*	jewel of the sea
Ullah *(H)*	a burden
Ulrica *(T)*	rule of all
Una *(L)*	the one
Undine *(L)*	water nymph
Unity *(ME)*	unity
Urania *(G)*	heavenly; celestial
Uria *(H)*	light of the Lord
Ursula *(L)*	little she-bear

V

Valda *(T)*	battle heroine
Valentina *(L)*	vigorous
Valerie *(L)*	} strong
Valery	
Vanessa *(G)*	butterfly
Vania *(H)*	God's gracious gift
Vashti *(H)*	fairest; loveliest
Veba *(San)*	wise
Velda *(T)*	of great wisdom
Velma *(T)*	warm-hearted
Vera *(Russ)*	faith
Verda *(L)*	young; fresh
Verna *(L)*	spring-born
Veronica *(L)*	true image
Vesta *(L)*	guardian of the sacred fire
Victoria *(L)*	} victorious
Victorine	
Vida *(HL)*	beloved
Vinna *(OE)*	of the vine
Violet *(L)*	} shy; modest
Viola	
Virginia *(L)*	pure; chaste
Vita *(L)*	life
Vivian *(L)*	} lively
Vivienne	

The use of the familiar form of a name can make a significant difference. Imagine famous vamp Theda Bara being called her full first name: Theodosia.

W

Wallis *(T)*	girl of Wales	Wilda *(AS)*	untamed wild one
Wanda *(T)*	wanderer	Wileen *(T)*	resolute protectress
Wendy	familiar form of Gwendolyn	Wilfreda *(T)*	resolute peacemaker
		Wilhelmina *(T)*	protectress
Wenona *(Am. Ind.)*	the first born	Willa *(AS)*	desired; desirable
		Wilma *(T)*	determined
Wesley *(OE)*	from the west meadow	Winifred *(T)*	friend of peace
		Wynne *(C)*	fair; white

X

Xanthe *(G)*	blonde	Xena *(G)*	hospitable
Xantippe *(G)*	shrewish	Xenia	
		Xylia *(G)*	of the wood

Y

Yetta *(T)*	mistress of the house	Yoshiko *(J)*	good
Yolande *(L)*	modest; shy	Yvonne *(F)*	the archer
Yolanda		Yvette	

Z

Zabrina *(AS)*	of the nobility	Zillah *(H)*	restful
Zada *(A)*	lucky one	Zinah *(H)*	abundance
Zandra *(G)*	helper of mankind	Zipporah *(H)*	bird
Zaneta *(H)*	God's gracious gift	Zita *(G)*	harvester
Zebada *(H)*	gift of the Lord	Zoe *(G)*	life
Zelda	short form of Griselda	Zola *(It)*	earthball
Zenda *(P)*	womanly	Zora *(L)*	
Zena *(G)*	} hospitable	Zorah	} dawn
Zenia		Zorana	
Zenobia *(G)*	having life from Jupiter	Zsa Zsa	Hungarian form of Susan
Zerlina *(T)*	serenely beautiful	Zuleika *(A)*	fair

Text design by Holly Johnson.

*The type faces used in this book
are Galliard and Zapf
International Demi.*